LIBERALISM AND DEMOCRACY

LIBERALISM AND DEMOCRACY

Norberto Bobbio
Translated by Martin Ryle and Kate Soper

VERSO
London • New York

Originally published as *Liberalismo e democrazia* by
Franco Angeli Libri, Milan 1988
© Franco Angeli Libri 1988
Translation first published by Verso 1990
© Verso 1990
This edition published by Verso 2005

The moral rights of the author and translator have been asserted

3 5 7 9 10 8 6 4 2

Verso
UK: 6 Meard Street, London W1F 0EG
USA: 20 Jay St, Suite 1010, Brooklyn, NY 11201
www.versobooks.com

Verso is the imprint of New Left Books

ISBN: 978-1-84467-062-8

British Library Cataloguing in Publication Data
A catalogue record for this book is available from the British Library

Library of Congress Cataloging-in-Publication Data
A catalog record for this book is available from the Library of Congress

Contents

1

Classical and Modern Ideas of Liberty

The existence at the present time of regimes referred to as 'liberal-democratic' or 'democratic-liberal' suggests that liberalism and democracy are interdependent. In reality, however, the relationship between the two is very complex and by no means one of continuity or identity. In the commonest usage of the two terms, 'liberalism' denotes a particular conception of the state, in which the state is conceived as having limited powers and functions, and thus as differing from both the absolute state and from what is nowadays called the social state; 'democracy' denotes one of many possible modes of government, namely that in which power is not vested in a single individual or in the hands of a few, but lies with everybody, or rather with the majority. Democracy is thus differentiated from autocratic forms such as monarchy and oligarchy. A liberal state is not necessarily democratic: indeed, there are historical instances of liberal states in societies where participation in government was highly restricted, and limited to the wealthy classes. A democratic government does not necessarily issue in a liberal state: indeed, the classical liberal state now finds itself in crisis as a result of the progressive democratization that has followed on the gradual extension of the franchise to the point where it has become universal.

In his comparison of modern and ancient ideas of liberty, Benjamin Constant (1767–1830) counterposed liberalism to democracy, discussing the distinction between the two with some subtlety in his celebrated address to the Royal Academy in Paris in 1818. This provides a starting-point for tracing the history of the vexed and controversial relations between the fundamental demands that have given rise to the contemporary forms of the state in the most economically and socially developed nations: the demand, on the one hand, that power should be limited; and on the other, that it be distributed. He writes:

> The ancients aimed at a distribution of power among all the citizens of a given state, and they referred to this as freedom. For the moderns, the goal is security in their private possessions. For them, liberty refers to the guarantees of these possessions afforded by their institutions.[1]

As a thoroughgoing liberal, Constant held that these two aims were mutually incompatible. Where everyone participates directly in collective decisions, the individual ends up being subordinated to the authority of the whole, and loses his liberty as a private person; and it is private liberty which the citizen today demands of public power. Hence, he concludes:

> We today are no longer able to enjoy the liberty of the ancients, which consisted in their continual and active participation in collective power. Our freedom, by contrast, must reside in the peaceful enjoyment of private independence.[2]

Although Constant cites the ancients, his argument is directed at a figure closer in time: Jean-Jacques Rousseau. The author of *The Social Contract*, drawing heavily on classical authors, had in fact envisaged a republic in which sovereign power, once constituted by universal voluntary agreement, would become infallible and 'need give no guarantee to its subjects, because it is impossible for the body to wish to hurt all its members'.[3] To be sure, Rousseau never took the argument of the general will so far as to deny the necessity of limiting state power: it is as misconceived as it is common-place to charge him with being the founder of 'totalitarian democracy'. Although he maintained that the social pact endows the body politic with an absolute power, he also insisted that 'the sovereign, for its part, cannot impose upon its subjects any fetters that are useless to the community'.[4] It is true, however, that these limits are not established prior to the birth of the state, as is the case in the doctrine of natural rights which provides the core of the thinking behind the liberal state. Rousseau, indeed, while he admits that 'each man alienates ... by the social contract, only such part of his powers ... as it is important for the community to control', concludes nonetheless that 'it must also be granted that the Sovereign is sole judge of what is important'.[5]

2

The Rights of Man

The philosophical presupposition of the liberal state, understood as the limited state and counterposed to the absolute
state, is to be found in the doctrine of natural rights developed
by the school of natural rights (or natural law). This holds that
man – all persons without exception – possesses by nature, and
thus irrespective of his own will and still more so of the will
of one or a few others, certain fundamental rights, such as the
right to life, liberty, security and happiness. The state, or more
concretely those who at a given time enjoy the legitimate
power to enforce obedience to their commands, must respect
these rights, must not infringe them and must guarantee them
against any possible transgression by others. To attribute a
right to someone is to recognize that the individual in question
has the *capacity* to act or not to act just as he pleases, and also
the *power* to resist, availing himself in the last instance of the
use of force (his own or others'), against whoever may trans-
gress that right: so that potential transgressors have in turn a
duty (or *obligation*) to abstain from any action which might
interfere in any way with this capacity to act or not to act.
'Rights' and 'duties' are notions carrying prescriptive force,
and as such they presuppose the existence of a norm or rule of

conduct which in the same moment as it recognizes the capacity of the subject to act or not act as he pleases also requires everyone else to abstain from all acts which might in any way hinder the exercise of that capacity. One might define the natural law doctrine as asserting the existence of laws not established by human will, and which accordingly precede the formation of any social group: such laws can be ascertained by rational enquiry, and from them, as from all moral or juridical laws, rights and duties derive which, in virtue of their derivation from a natural law, are natural rights and duties. We have spoken of the doctrine of natural law as the 'philosophical' presupposition of liberalism because it serves to establish the limits of power on the basis of a general and hypothetical conception of the nature of man, which dispenses with any kind of empirical verification and historical proof. In his second *Treatise of Government*, Locke, one of the fathers of modern liberalism, takes as his starting-point the state of nature which he describes as a state of perfect liberty and equality, governed by a law of nature which 'teaches all mankind who will but consult it, that being all equal and independent, no one might do harm to another in his life, health, liberty or possessions'.[6]

This description is the outcome of an imaginary reconstruction of a presumed original state of man, and its sole purpose is to allow Locke a good reason to justify limiting the power of the state. The doctrine of natural rights in fact underlies the North American Declaration of Independence (1776) and the Declaration of the Rights of Man of the French Revolution (1789), in both of which we find an affirmation of the fundamental principle of the liberal state as a limited state: 'The aim of every political association is the preservation of the natural and imprescriptible rights of man' (Article Two of the Declaration of the Rights of Man and of the Citizen, 1789).

As a theory variously developed by philosophers, theologians and jurists, the doctrine of the rights of man can be regarded as a later rationalization of the state of affairs resulting from the struggle many centuries earlier, especially in England, between the king and other social forces. In the Magna Carta, to which King John yielded his consent in 1215, we find a recognition of what in future centuries were to be called the 'rights of man': these are designated as 'liberties' (*libertates, franchises,* freedoms), or as recognized spheres of individual action and property in goods which are protected against the coercive power of the king. Although the charter and its successors may have taken the juridical form of sovereign concessions, they were in reality the outcome of a genuine pact between opposing parties. The pact, commonly known as the *pactum subjectionis,* concerns reciprocal rights and duties in the political relationship: in the relationship, that is, between the duty (of the sovereign) to protect and the duty (of the subject) to obey (his so-called 'political obligation'). The principal object of a charter of 'liberties' is to define forms and limits of obedience, or, in other words, of the subject's political obligation and the corresponding forms and limits of the sovereign's right to command. These ancient charters, like the constitutional charters granted – *octroyées* – by constitutional monarchies during the restoration period and since (which include the Albertine constitution of 1848), admittedly take the juridical form of a unilateral concession on the part of the monarch, even though in reality they are the result of bilateral accord. However, this is no more than a typical legal fiction, whose purpose is to safeguard the principle of the king's supremacy and to ensure the maintenance of the monarchical form of government, despite the limitations actually imposed on the traditional powers of the holder of supreme power.

Here, too, of course, we have another instance of a reverse presentation of the sequence between the historical events and the juridical agreement and rational justification to which they give rise: historically, the liberal state was the outcome of a continual and ever-growing erosion of the sovereign's absolute power, and of the revolutionary rupture which occurred in historical periods of sharper crisis (such as the seventeenth century in England and the late eighteenth century in France); rationally, it was justified as the outcome of an accord between individuals who are initially free and who come together to establish the bonds essential to a permanent and peaceful coexistence. The course of history led from an initial state of servitude, by way of a gradual process of liberalization, to the conquest by the subject of growing areas of liberty, but the doctrine proceeds in the opposite direction: only by taking as its starting-point a hypothetical initial state of liberty, and conceiving of man as naturally free, does it arrive at the construction of a political society as a society in which sovereignty is limited. Thus it is that the doctrine – here the doctrine of natural rights – inverts the course of historical events, treating as origin or foundation, as *prius*, that which is historically the result, which occurs *posterius*.

There is a close connection between the assertion of natural rights and the theory of the social contract, or contract theory. The idea that the exercise of political power is legitimate only if it is founded on the consent of those who are subject to it (another of Locke's theses), and thus that it is based on an agreement *among* those who decide to subject themselves to a higher power and *with* those to whom the exercise of power is entrusted, derives from the postulate that individuals possess rights not dependent on the institution of sovereignty and that the chief function of that institution is to allow the fullest possible realization of those rights compatible with secure social life. The connecting link between the doctrine of the rights of man and contract theory is the individualistic conception of society they hold in common: a conception according to which the particular individual, with his interests and needs, which take the form of rights in virtue of the acceptance of a hypothetical law of nature, comes first and precedes the establishment of society. This contrasts with the organicist conception, in all its various guises, which takes the opposite view, seeing society as prior to the individual, or the social whole as taking precedence over its parts (in the Aristotelian formulation which had so enduring an influence). Modern contract theory is a real turning-point in the history of political thought, dominated as it had been by the organic idea, insofar as the contract theorists reversed the relationship between individual and society, and no longer saw society as a natural fact existing independently of the will of individuals, but as an artificial body, created by individuals in their own image and likeness to promote the satisfaction of their own interests and needs and the fullest exercise of their rights. The agreement which gives birth to the state is in turn viewed as possible, according to the theory of natural right, in virtue of the law of nature which attributes to all individuals certain natural rights that can be enjoyed only in the context of the free and ordered form of coexistence secured through such a voluntary accord – an accord requiring a mutual and reciprocal renunciation of certain rights on the part of all the individuals concerned.

Without this Copernican revolution, which allowed the problem of the state to be viewed for the first time through the eyes of its subjects rather than its sovereign, the doctrine of the liberal state, which is first and foremost the doctrine of juridical limits to state power, would have been impossible. Without individualism, there can be no liberalism.

3

The Limits of State Power

Thus far, we have been speaking in general terms of the limited state or the limits to the state. It must now be made clear that such expressions cover two different aspects of the problem, which are not always properly distinguished: the limits (a) of the *powers*, and (b) of the *functions* of the state. Liberal doctrine includes both these aspects, even though they can be treated separately, each to the exclusion of the other. Liberalism refers us to limits both in the power and in the functions of the state. In respect of the limits of power one speaks currently of the *rights-based state*, while the term *minimal state* is used in reference to the limit on function. Even though liberalism conceives of the state as both rights-based and minimal, one can have rights-based, non-minimalist states (as with the social state today), and also minimalist states which are not rights-based (as is the case with Hobbes's Leviathan, in the economic sphere: a state which is at one and the same time absolute in the fullest sense of the term, and liberal in its economics). While the rights-based state is counterposed to the absolute state understood in the sense of *legibus solutus*, the minimal state is counterposed to the maximal state: and so we say that it is in the name of the liberal state that the struggle to defend the rights-based against the absolute state is waged, as that in defence of the minimal against the maximal state, even though the two emancipatory impulses do not always coincide in history and in practice.

The rights-based state is generally understood as a state in which public power is regulated by general norms (fundamental or constitutional laws) and must be exercised within the framework of the laws which regulate it, while citizens have secure rights of recourse to an independent judiciary in order to establish and prevent any abuse or excessive exercise of power. The rights-based state, understood in this sense, is a reflection of the old doctrine, going back to classical times and transmitted by way of medieval political theory, that the government of law is superior to the government of men, or as the formula has it, *lex facit regem* (the 'law makes the king').[7] Even in the period of absolutism, this doctrine survived, in that the maxim *princeps legibus solutus* ('the ruler is above the law')[8] was understood to mean that the sovereign, while exempt from the positive laws that he himself promulgated, remained subject to divine or natural laws and the fundamental laws of the kingdom. When we discuss the rights-based state in the context of the liberal account of the state, we must however add a further qualification to the traditional definition, namely the constitutional formulation of natural rights, or in other words the transformation of these rights into rights protected by law and thus into positive rights in the proper sense. In liberal doctrine, the rights-based state means not only that public power of every kind is subject to the general laws of the country (a purely formal limitation), but also that the laws themselves are subject to the material limitation stemming from the recognition of certain fundamental rights which are constitutionally, and thus as a matter of principle, taken to be 'inviolable' (the epithet is found in Article Two of the Italian constitution). From this point of view, we can distinguish the rights-based state in the strong sense from the weak sense in which it is the non-despotic state, ruled by laws rather than by men, and from an even weaker sense, that of Kelsen, for whom every state figures as a rights-based state, once reduced to its juridical ordinances; a definition which deprives the notion of a rights-based state of all descriptive force.

In the strong sense of the term, which is that intended by liberal doctrine, the rights-based state acquires its definitive character from all those constitutional mechanisms which obstruct or hinder the arbitrary or illegitimate exercise of power and prevent or discourage its abuse or illegal exercise. The most important of these mechanisms are: (1) the subordination of the executive to the legislative power, or to be more exact, of the government from which executive power proceeds to the parliament from which legislative power, and the power of political direction, derive in the last instance; (2) the ultimate accountability of parliament, in its exercise of ordinary legislative power, to a jurisdictional court to which is entrusted the entire constitutional aspect of legislation; (3) the relative autonomy of local government in all its forms and levels vis-à-vis central government; (4) a magistrature independent of the political authority.

4

Liberty versus Power

The constitutional mechanisms which characterize the rights-based state are intended to defend the individual against abuses of power. They are, in other words, guarantees of liberty, taking liberty in the sense of what is known as negative liberty – as a sphere of action within which the individual is neither constrained, by whoever holds the power of coercion, to do anything he does not wish to do, nor prevented from doing what he does wish to do. There is a sense (predominant in the liberal tradition) in which 'liberty' and 'power' can be counterposed as antithetical terms, denoting two realms which are mutually conflicting and thus incompatible. In the relationship between two persons, as the power of the former is enlarged (power, that is, to compel or forbid), so the liberty, that is the negative liberty, of the latter diminishes; and conversely, as the latter enlarges his sphere of liberty, the power of the former diminishes. We must now add that in liberal thought individual liberty is guaranteed, not only by the constitutional mechanisms of the rights-based state, but also by the fact that the state is entrusted only with those tasks involved in maintaining public order, domestically and internationally. In liberal thought, the theory of the need to control power and the theory of the limitation of the role of the state proceed *pari passu*. One may even claim that the second is the *sine qua non* of the first, in the sense that the abuse of power is that much more easily contained, the less space there is for the state to intervene. To put the matter in a nutshell, the minimal state is more controllable than the maximal state. From the individual's point of view, upon which liberalism is premised, the state is a necessary evil: and in being an evil, albeit a necessary one (here liberalism differs from anarchism), it should interfere as little as possible in the sphere of action of individuals. Thomas Paine (1737–1809), defending the rights of man on the eve of the American Revolution, expresses the viewpoint very clearly:

> Society is produced by our wants, and government by our wickedness; the former promotes our happiness *positively* by uniting our affections, the latter *negatively* by restraining our vices. The one encourages intercourse, the other creates distinctions. The first is a patron, the last a punisher. Society in every state is a blessing, but government even in its best state is but a necessary evil; in its worst state, an intolerable one.[9]

Once liberty has been given the definition which prevails in liberal doctrine – once it has been defined as liberty *from the state* – then the formation of the liberal state can be seen as coinciding with the gradual expansion of the sphere in which the individual is free from interference by the public powers (to use Paine's term), or with the gradual emancipation of society or of civil society, in the Hegelian or Marxist sense, from the state. The two chief spheres of this emancipation are those, on the one hand, of religion and spiritual matters generally, and on the other of economic life or material concerns. Weber, in his well-known thesis on the relation between the protestant ethic and the spirit of capitalism, argued that the two processes were closely connected. It is, at all events, a fact that the history of the liberal states coincides both with the demise of confessional states and the rise of states neutral or agnostic in their attitude to the religious beliefs of their citizens; and with the demise of the privileges and bonds of feudalism and the emergence of the demand for free disposal of wealth and liberty of exchange, which marks the birth and development of the bourgeois mercantile society.

Viewed in this perspective, the liberal state must be seen as distinct from any form of paternalism. From the paternalist point of view, the duty of the state is to care for its subjects after the manner in which a father cares for his children, a form of solicitude justified by the supposedly permanent minority status of its subjects. One of Locke's aims in the *Two Treatises of Civil Government* was to demonstrate that the civil power, created to guarantee the liberty and property of individuals who have formed an association for governing themselves, is distinct from paternal governance and hence, *a fortiori*, from patronage. It is thus against paternalism that Kant (1724–1804), for his part, most clearly and effectively takes aim, when he observes that

> a government founded on the principle of benevolence towards the people, like the governance of a father over his children, in other words, a paternalistic government (*imperium paternale*), in which the subjects, like minors who cannot distinguish between what is good and what is bad for them, are forced to adopt a passive role, and must look to the sovereign to determine the nature of their happiness, expecting nothing except what he chooses to bestow on them: such a government is the worst possible despotism one can imagine.[10]

Kant's primary concern is with the moral freedom of the individual. In the field of economic freedom and material self-interest, Adam Smith's concerns are equally clear and pronounced: in accordance with 'the system of natural freedom' the sovereign has no more than three significant responsibilities, namely, the defence of society against external enemies, the protection of each individual against any harm inflicted upon him by another, and the undertaking of such public works as would not be carried out if entrusted to private profit. For Kant, as for Smith, despite their very differing starting-points, the limitation of the role of the state is grounded in the prior liberty of the individual relative to the power of the sovereign, and thus on the subordination of the latter's duties to the rights or interests of the individual.

At the close of the century of the Declarations of Rights, the century of Kant and Smith, Wilhelm von Humboldt (1767–1835) perfectly summed up the liberal ideal of the state in his *The Limits of State Action* (1792). The author's intention, already plain in the essay's title, is further displayed in the epigraph to the first chapter, which is drawn from the elder Mirabeau:

> The hard thing is to promulgate only such laws as are necessary, and to remain ever faithful to the authentic constitutional principle of society, which demands of governments that they constrain their fury to govern, this being the deadliest disease afflicting modern regimes.

It is Humboldt's unswerving conviction that the individual, in his ineffable particularity and variety, must be the starting-point. Man's true end, he states, is to develop his faculties as fully as possible. If this end is to be attained, then the state should be guided ideally by the following principle:

> That reason cannot desire for man any other condition than that in which each individual not only enjoys the most absolute freedom of developing himself by his own energies, in his perfect individuality, but in which external nature itself is left unfashioned by any human agency, but only receives the impress given to it by each individual by himself and of his own free will according to the measure of his wants and instincts, and restricted only by the limits of his powers and his rights.[11]

From this premise, Humboldt draws the conclusion that 'any state interference in private affairs, where there is no immediate reference to violence done to individual rights, should be absolutely condemned'.[12] This inversion of the traditional, organicist view of the relation between individual and state, is paralleled and reinforced by a further inversion directly bearing upon it, that of means and end: the state, according to Humboldt, is not an end in itself, but merely a means 'to raise the culture of the citizen to such a point that he may find every incentive to cooperation in the state's designs, in the consciousness of the advantages which the political institutions offer his own individual interests'.[13] If the state does have an ultimate end, it is 'security'. It is repeatedly stated in Humboldt's essay that the purpose of the state is simply 'security', defined as 'the assurance of legal freedom'.[14]

5

The Fruitfulness of Conflict

As well as presenting individual liberty as the sole end of the state and arguing that the state is a means rather than an end in itself, Humboldt's writings have another thematic motif of great interest to any analysis of liberal thought, namely their praise of 'variety'. In a closely argued critique of the 'providential state', the state which manifests an excessive solicitude for the 'well-being' of its citizens, Humboldt (whose line of argument anticipates contemporary neo-liberal denunciations of the supposed ill effects of the welfare state) explains that when government intervenes outside its allotted sphere of action, the maintenance of internal and external order, the result is to create uniformity of behaviour in society and thus to stifle the natural variety of character and temperament. Governments, in despite of individuals, seek an undisturbed state of well-being: 'but what man does and must have in view is something quite different – it is variety and activity'.[15] Those who think otherwise may justly be suspected of regarding men as automata. 'Hence it arises,' he adds (and what would Humboldt's reaction have been to the 'steel cage' of the modern bureaucratic state?), 'that in most states from decade to decade the number of the public officials and the extent of registration increase, while the liberty of the subject proportionately declines'.[16] And he concludes: 'in the kind of policy we are supposing, then, men are neglected for things, and creature powers for results'.[17]

In defending the individual against the presumptions of the state which would provide for his well-being, one is therefore touching on matters not only of material interest but also of morality. We are nowadays so accustomed to an exclusively economic critique of the welfare state that it is hard to recapture a sense of the strong ethical charge carried by early liberalism, and to remember that the critique of paternalism had as its principal raison d'être the defence of the individual's autonomy. In this respect, there is a line of linkage between Humboldt and Kant, and between both thinkers and Constant. For Smith, too, who was moreover a moralist before he became an economist, liberty has its moral value.

Associated with its counterposing of individual variety to state-sponsored uniformity, we discover a further original and characteristic theme of liberal thought: the insistence that conflict is fruitful. Traditional organicist views of society had put harmony at a premium: concord, even if it necessitated compulsion, was a good; the parts must be subordinated to the whole in a regulated and ordered fashion, and conflict was to be condemned as a factor of disruption and social disintegration. In all those currents of thought which set themselves against organicism, we find a growing emphasis on the idea that opposition between individuals and groups (and between nations, too, whence the praise of warfare as a nurse of popular virtue) is beneficent, being a necessary condition of humanity's technical and moral progress. This progress is seen as brought about solely through the clash of divergent opinions and interests, through conflicts which in the realm of argument further the quest for truth; which in economic competition tend to secure the greatest social prosperity; and whose struggles in the political domain result in the selection of those best fitted to govern. On the basis of such a general conception of mankind and its history, it is no mystery if individual liberty – conceived as an emancipation from the chains in which for centuries individuals had been imprisoned by tradition, custom, and authorities both religious and secular – came to be viewed as the essential condition allowing the realization of the 'variety' of individual personalities to be viewed as compatible with conflict, and conflict itself as promoting the perfection of all.

In his essay on 'The Idea of Universal History from a Cosmopolitan Point of View' (1784), Kant expresses, in as unprejudicial a fashion as possible, his conviction that antagonism is 'the means used by nature to further the development of all her dispositions',[18] and by 'antagonism' he means man's tendency to satisfy his own interests in competition with those of everyone else – a tendency which awakens all his energies, leads him to overcome his propensity to indolence, and encourages him to strive for eminence among his fellows. Comparing the antagonistic to the harmonious society from the point of view of its moral as well as economic significance, Kant delivers himself of a judgement which might well be viewed as capturing the heart of liberal thinking: 'In the absence of unsociability, all human talents would remain confined to an embryonic stage within an Arcadian pastoral existence; men, like the obedient sheep under the shepherd's guidance, would ascribe no value whatsoever to their life'. And on the basis of this explosive judgement he offers the following hymn in praise of the wisdom of creation:

> Let thanks be given to nature for the stubbornness she engenders, the invidious and vainglorious spirit of emulation, the never sated greed for wealth – and for power too! For without her, all the excellent natural human dispositions would remain forever dormant and deprived of development.[19]

As a theory of the limited state, liberalism counterposes the rights-based state to the absolute state and the minimal to the

maximal state. The theory of progress as mediated by antagonism introduces a further opposition, between the free states
of Europe and the despotisms of the Orient. 'Despotism' is a
term dating back to antiquity, and alongside its descriptive
meaning it has always had a strong polemical connotation. As
liberal thought expanded, 'despotism' acquired an additional
negative charge: since despotic states plunge everyone into
subjugation (so that, as Machiavelli had put it, the entire
monarchy of the Turk is 'governed by one lord, the others are
his servants',[20] or, as Hegel (1770–1831) said of the despotic
regimes of the Orient, 'only one man is free'[21]), they also tend
towards stagnation and inertia. The law of indefinite progress
does not apply to them, but is valid only of civilized Europe.
From this point of view, in addition to figuring as a general
political category, the liberal state becomes a criterion of
historical interpretation.

6

Ancient and Modern Ideas of Democracy

As a theory of the state (and also as a key to the interpretation of history), liberalism is modern, whereas democracy as a form of government is ancient. Democracy figures in the famous typology of modes of government bequeathed to us by Greek political thought, by which it is defined as government by the many or by most or by the majority or by the poor (but where the poor have obtained the upper hand, this indicates that power belongs to the *pleithos*, to the masses). In short, democracy, as its etymology tells us, is government by the people, as opposed to government by one or by a few. Whatever may be said, and despite the passage of centuries and the innumerable arguments that have taken place about the difference between the democracy of the ancients and that of the moderns, the general descriptive significance of the term has not changed, though its evaluative load has altered with changing times and beliefs, and in response to the degree of support for popular as opposed to monarchical or oligarchical government. What is held to have changed in the passage from ancient to modern democracy, at any rate in the view of those who find the distinction a useful one, is not the people's entitlement to political power (where by 'people' is meant the entire body of citizens with whom the right to take collective decisions ultimately rests), but the ways in which it is exercised, which may be more or less extensive at any given point. In the same period which saw the Declarations of Rights, we find the authors of *The Federalist* opposing the direct democracy that prevailed in antiquity and in medieval city-states to the representative democracy which is the only mode of popular government possible in a large state. Hamilton puts it as follows:

> It is impossible to read the history of the petty republics of Greece and Italy without feeling sensations of horror and disgust at the distractions with which they were continually agitated, and at the rapid succession of revolutions by which they were kept in a state of perpetual vibration between the extremes of tyranny and anarchy.[22]

A judgement which Madison echoes: 'The friend of popular governments never finds himself so alarmed for their character and fate as when he contemplates their propensity to this dangerous vice'.[23] The claim that the democracy of the city-state was flawed by its tendency to factionalism was in fact no more than a pretext, a harking back to the longstanding and recurrent contempt for the people felt by oligarchic groups: had there been representative assemblies, the division into mutually opposed groups would have been expressed in the formation of parties. The single reason of any weight for favouring representative democracy lay in the sheer size of the modern state; an early instance was the union of thirteen English colonies whose new constitution the contributors to *The Federalist* were discussing. Rousseau himself, passionate admirer of the ancients as he was, had recognized as much. He had indeed defended direct democracy, holding that 'sovereignty ... cannot be represented' and that for this reason, although 'the people of England regards itself as free', it is 'grossly mistaken; it is free only during the election of members of parliament. As soon as they are elected, slavery overtakes it, and it is nothing'.[24] However, he was also convinced that 'there has never been a real democracy, and there never will be', because it presupposes first a very small state 'where the people can readily be got together'; secondly, 'a great simplicity of manners'; next, 'a large measure of equality in rank and fortune'; and lastly, 'little or no luxury'. Hence, he was persuaded that if 'there were a people of gods, their government would be democratic. So perfect a government is not for men'.[25]

Both the authors of *The Federalist* and the French Constituent Assemblies were convinced that the only kind of democratic government suitable for a population of human beings was representative democracy, that form of government in which the people does not itself take the decisions which affect it but elects its own representatives to decide on its behalf. However, the institution of representative democracy was certainly not regarded by them as a diminution of the principle of popular government. One proof of this may be found in the constitution of the State of Virginia (1776), the first written constitution of any North American state, which asserts – and the same formula recurs in later constitutions – that: 'All power resides with the people, and in consequence derives from it; the magistrates are the peoples' trustees and servants, and at all times responsible towards them'. So, too, Article Three of the 1789 Declaration: 'The principle of every sovereignty resides essentially within the nation. No body, no individual, can exercise authority which does not derive expressly from it'. Quite apart from the fact that the direct exercise of power by the citizens is not incompatible with its direct exercise by way of elected representatives (as is demonstrated by the existence of constitutions such as that now observed in Italy, where provision is made for popular referenda, though these can only veto or annul legislation), direct and indirect democracy can both be traced back to some principle of popular sovereignty, even if they differ in the modes and forms by which that sovereignty is exercised.

Representative democracy was fostered also by the conviction that the citizens' elected representatives would be better able to judge the common interest than the citizens themselves, whose vision would be too narrowly focused on their particular interests. Representative democracy might even for these reasons be better suited to achieving the ends envisaged by popular sovereignty. This would mean again that it is ultimately misleading to counterpose ancient and modern democracy, at least in the sense that the former is a more perfect form in respect of these ends. Madison maintained that the delegation of governmental power to a small number of men of proven wisdom would put the 'true interest' of the country in the hands of those 'least likely to sacrifice it to temporary or partial considerations'.[26] This depended upon the deputy's behaving, once he was elected, not as the confidential agent of those electors who had put him in parliament, but as a representative of the whole nation. If democracy was to be representative in the proper sense of the term, the elected representative could no longer be bound by the will of the electorate – a form of dependency characteristic, in fact, of the old society of rank and caste, in which various groups, corporations and collective bodies had used their delegates as a means of transmission to the sovereign of their own particular demands. Here, too, England led the way. As Burke wrote:

> To deliver an opinion is the right of all men, that of constituents is a weighty and respectable opinion, which a representative might always rejoice to hear.... But *authoritative* instructions, *mandates* issued, which the member is bound blindly and implicitly to obey, to vote, and to argue for, ... these are things utterly unknown to the laws of this land.[27]

The French Constituent Assemblies, acting on the eloquently expressed opinion of Siéyès (1748–1836), made provision in the 1791 constitution (tit. III, ch. I, sect. III, art. 7) for a formally binding separation between representative and those represented: the relevant article, proscribing any binding mandate, lays it down that 'the nominated representatives in the *départements* shall not be representatives of a particular *département*, but of the whole nation, and cannot be mandated by it'.[28] From then on, it became one of the essential principles of the functioning of the parliamentary system that representatives were forbidden to accept any binding mandate from those who had elected them. This principle, indeed, was what distinguished parliamentary government from the previous state of affairs in which the opposite principle of corporative representation had applied, based on binding mandates which institutionally compelled delegates to further the interests of the corporation they represented and, should they show any disinclination to do so, deprived them of their rights as representatives. The disappearance of the corporative state left individuals free in their particularity and autonomy: it was individuals as such, and not as members of any corporation, who were charged with electing the nation's representatives. Those elected were in turn called upon by the particular individuals who elected them to represent the nation as a whole, and they therefore had to determine their course of action and take their decisions unfettered by any mandate. If by modern democracy we mean representative democracy, and if it is of the essence of the latter that the representatives of the nation are not directly obliged to the particular individuals they represent nor to their particular interests, then modern democracy is premised upon the atomization of the nation and its recomposition at another level – the level of parliamentary assemblies, which is at once higher and more restricted. Now this process of atomization is the same which underlies the liberal conception of the state, whose foundation, as we have argued, is to be sought in the assertion of the individual's natural and inviolable rights.

7

Democracy and Equality

Modern liberalism and ancient democracy have often been regarded as antithetical. The democrats of antiquity were ignorant of both the doctrine of natural rights and the idea that the state had a duty to confine its activities to the minimum necessary for the community's survival; the liberals of modern times, for their part, were from the outset extremely suspicious of all forms of popular government (throughout the nineteenth century, and later, they upheld and defended limited suffrage). Modern democracy, however, is not only not incompatible with liberalism, but can in many respects, if only to a degree, be regarded as its natural extension.

But this is true only if we take the term 'democracy' in its juridical–institutional rather than its ethical sense – if we take it in a more procedural than substantial sense. There is no question that historically the term 'democracy' has been interpreted, at least in its origins, in either one of two main senses, depending on whether the stress is laid more on the body of rules (the 'rules of the game') which must be observed if political power is to be effectively distributed among the majority of the citizens, or on the ideal of equality in which democratic government should find its inspiration. In observance of this distinction, it has been customary to differentiate between formal and substantial democracy, or, as it is otherwise commonly put, between government by the people and government for the people. Needless to say, the term 'democracy' is here being used in two such differing senses that it is bound to issue in useless controversy of the kind surrounding the question as to which is more democratic, a regime wherein formal democracy is found without widespread equality or one in which widespread equality is achieved by way of despotic government. Either sense has historical legitimation, for in the long history of the theory of democracy, procedural questions are interwoven with ideals (the two are fused only in Rousseau's theory, whose strongly egalitarian ideal is conceived as realizable only through the formation of the general will). However, the fact that history allows both uses sheds no light on what connotations they may come to share.

Of the two senses in question, it is the first which is linked historically with the formation of the liberal state. When democracy is taken in its second sense, the problems of its relationship to liberalism are rendered very complex. There is no reason to suppose any immediate end to the inconclusive debates which have been already been conducted around these problems. Indeed, when conceived in this light the question of the relation between liberalism and democracy resolves itself into the difficult problem of the relation between liberty and equality, which assumes that we can offer unequivocal answers to the questions: 'What kind of liberty? What kind of equality?'

In their broadest significance, that they acquire through the extension of the respective demands for rights to liberty and equality (the demands of the opposed doctrines of laissez-faire and egalitarianism) into the economic sphere, liberty and equality are antithetical values, in the sense that neither can be fully realized except at the expense of the other: a liberal laissez-faire society is inevitably inegalitarian, and an egalitarian society is inevitably illiberal. Libertarianism and egalitarianism are rooted in profoundly divergent conceptions of man and society – conceptions which are individualistic, conflictual and pluralistic for the liberal; totalizing, harmonious and monistic for the egalitarian. The chief goal for the liberal is the expansion of the individual personality, even if the wealthier and more talented achieve this development at the expense of that of the poorer and less gifted. The chief goal for the egalitarian is the enhancement of the community as a whole, even if this entails some constriction of the sphere of individual freedom.

There is one form only of equality – equality in the right to liberty – which is not only compatible with liberalism but actually demanded by its view of freedom. Equality in liberty means that each person should enjoy as much liberty as is compatible with the liberty of others, and may do anything which does not distrain on the equal liberty of others. This form of equality inspired, very early in the development of the liberal state, two fundamental principles that came to be expressed in constitutional provisions: (a) equality before the law, and (b) equality of rights. The former is found in the French constitutions of 1791, 1793 and 1795; it then appears in the 1814 Charter (art. 1), the Belgian constitution of 1813 (art. 6), and the Albertine Constitution of 1848 (art. 24). The Fourteenth Amendment to the Constitution of the United States, guaranteeing 'the equal protection of the law' to every citizen, has similar scope. The second principle is solemnly proclaimed in Article One of the 1789 Declaration of the Rights of Man and of the Citizen: 'Men are born and remain free and equal in their rights'. Both principles find expression all through the history of modern constitutionalism, and both are jointly expressed in clause 1 of Article Three of the current Italian constitution: 'All citizens enjoy equal social status and are equal before the law'.

The principle of equality before the law can be understood in a narrow sense as a reformulation of the principle obtaining in all courts and tribunals: 'The law is equal for all'. Understood in this sense, it means no more than that judges are to apply the law impartially, and as such is an integral component of the constitutional measures and procedures of the rights-based state: from which it follows that it is an inherent feature of the liberal state, the latter being identified, as we have argued, with the rights-based state. Understood in a wider sense, it is a principle of the universal application of the law to all citizens, and thus carries the implication that such laws as apply only to particular ranks of persons or their situations should be repealed or at any rate not renewed: the principle is an egalitarian one in that it does away with previous discrimination. The preamble to the 1791 Declaration informs us that the Constituent Assemblies have wanted to abolish 'irrevocably those institutions which are injurious to liberty and the equality of rights', and included among the institutions named are those most typically feudal. The concluding phrases of the Preamble state that 'There shall no longer be any section of the nation, nor any individual, who is accorded any privilege or excluded from common right of all French citizens'; and here, through the negative formulations of the text, we have the clearest possible illustration of the principle of equality before the law in its positive meaning as implying rejection of the society of rank and caste, and hence as affirming the conception of society as comprised originally of purely individual subjects (of individuals *uti singuli*).

Equality of rights represents, for its part, a further development of equality, which extends beyond the idea of equality before the law in the sense of universal exemption from the discriminations of the old society of rank. It involves the equal enjoyment by all citizens of certain fundamental, constitutionally guaranteed rights. Whereas equality before the law can be interpreted as a particular, historically determined form of juridical equality (comprising, for instance, the right of everyone, irrespective of birth, to have access to the common judicial system or to gain entry into the main civil and military careers), equality of rights comprises equality in all those fundamental rights enumerated in a given constitution, and implies that all such rights, and only those rights, may be considered fundamental, which every citizen enjoys without discrimination on the basis of social class, sex, religion, race, etc. The repertory of fundamental rights differs from one age to another and from one community to another, and thus no once-for-all list can be drawn up: we can say only that under a particular constitution, those rights are to be called fundamental which are attributed to all citizens without distinction – those, in a word, in respect of which all citizens are equal.

8

Liberalism's Encounter with Democracy

None of the principles of equality reviewed above, which are connected with the rise of the liberal state, has anything to do with democratic egalitarianism, whose scope extends to pursuit of the ideal of some degree of economic equalization, an ideal foreign to liberal thought. The latter has, over time, come to accept, in addition to juridical equality, equality of opportunity, which provides for parity between individuals in their point of departure, but not in their point of arrival. As concerns, then, various possible constructions that can be put on the notion of equality, liberalism and democracy have been destined to follow separate paths, and this explains why over a long period they were, historically, counterposed. In what sense, then, can democracy be seen as the extension and proper realization of the liberal state, thus justifying our use of the phrase 'liberal-democratic' to describe a number of present-day regimes? Not only is liberalism compatible with democracy, but democracy can be seen as the natural development of liberalism, providing that we have in mind not the ideal, egalitarian aspect of democracy, but its character as a political formula in which, as we have seen, it is tantamount to popular sovereignty. Popular sovereignty can only be effectively exercised if the majority of citizens are granted the right to participate directly and indirectly in collective decision-making: in other words, if there is a continuous extension of political rights to the point of universal male and female suffrage, the only restriction being that which stipulates a lower age limit (usually coinciding with the age of legal majority). Even though many liberal writers regarded the extension of the suffrage as ill-timed or undesirable, and even though during the period of the formation of the liberal state, only those who owned property were entitled to vote, universal suffrage is not in principle inconsistent with either the rights-based state or the minimal state. Such, then, was the inter-dependence between the two which gradually came to establish itself, that although at the outset it was possible for liberal states to come into being that were not democratic (except in their declarations of principle), today non-demo-cratic liberal states would be inconceivable, as would non-liberal democratic states. There are, in short, good reasons to believe that (a) the procedures of democracy are necessary to safeguard those fundamental personal rights on which the liberal state is based; and (b) those rights must be safeguarded if democratic procedures are to operate.

As concerns the first point, it should be noted that what best guarantees that rights to liberty will be protected against the tendency to limit and suppress them, on the part of those who govern, is the capacity of the citizen to defend those rights against possible abuse. Now the best available remedy against all possible forms of abuse of power (not that 'best available' signifies perfect, or infallible) is the direct or indirect particip-ation of citizens, and of the greatest possible number of citizens, in the formation of the laws. From this point of view, political rights are the natural corollary of rights to liberty: in the terms made famous by Jellinek (1851–1911), the *iura activae civitatis* ('rights of active citizenship') are the best safeguard of the *iura libertatis et civitatis* ('rights of liberty and citizenship'), while, in a regime not based on popular sovereignty, that safeguard depends solely on the natural rights of resistance to oppression.

In connection with the second point, and here we are concerned not with the necessity of democracy to the survival of the liberal state but rather with the need for inviolable personal rights to be recognized if democracy is to function well, we must remark that voting can be regarded as a proper and effective exercise of political power (that is, of the power to influence collective decisions) only if the vote is a free one, or, in other words, only if the individual who places his or her paper in the ballot box enjoys liberty of opinion, a free press, rights of free assembly and association, and all those liberties which are the essence of the liberal state, and which thus constitute necessary preconditions for a real rather than fictitious participation in the process of election.

Liberal ideals and democratic procedures have gradually become interwoven. While it is true that rights to liberty have from the beginning been a necessary condition for the proper application of the rules of the democratic game, it is equally true that the development of democracy has over time become the principal tool for the defence of rights to liberty. Today, the only democratic states are those which were born out of the liberal revolutions, and only in democratic states are the rights of man protected: every authoritarian state in the world is at once anti-liberal and anti-democratic.

9

Individualism and Organicism

This reciprocal relation between liberalism and democracy is possible because they share a common starting-point: the individual. Both are grounded in an individualistic conception of society. The entire history of political thought is riven by the great dichotomy between organicism (holism) and individualism (atomism). Though there is no unilinear pattern, we can say, roughly speaking, that organicism is ancient and classical, and individualism is modern (or at least that it is in individualism that the theory of the modern state finds its origin). This is closer to the truth than is Constant's historical counterposing of democracy (ancient) to liberalism (modern). For organicism, the state is a body, an overall corporate structure made up of parts, each of which has its own destiny, but which all cooperate in a relation of interdependence, to further their joint collective life: individuals *uti singuli* are not regarded as possessing any autonomy. Individualism sees the state as a collection of individuals, and as acquiring its form only through their actions and the relations they establish with one another. In the first pages of the *Politics*, Aristotle gives us the definitive formulation of the constitutive principles of organicism: 'The whole is necessarily prior to the part. If the whole body is destroyed, there will not be a foot or a head'. We thus see that 'the polis exists by nature and that it is prior to the individual'.[29] A complete and fully self-aware individualistic theory is not found until we come to Hobbes, who begins with the hypothesis of a state of nature in which there exist only individuals, separated from each other by their mutually opposed passions and interests, and obliged to come together by common consent in a political society in order to avoid mutual destruction. This reversal of the previous starting-point has decisive consequences for the birth of modern liberal and democratic thought. As far as liberalism is concerned, a coherent organic conception in which the state is held to be a totality anterior and superior to its parts can allow no space for spheres of action independent of the whole; it can recognize no distinction between private and public spheres, nor can it justify the abstraction of individual interests, satisfied in relations with other individuals (through the market), from the public interest. Democracy, for its part, is based on a conception of power as issuing from below, and regards organicism's contrary understanding of power as descending from above as an encouragement to autocratic models of government; it is difficult to imagine an organism under the command not of the head but of its members.

It must be added that while both liberalism and democracy are individualistic conceptions, the individual of the former is not the same as the individual of the latter, or to be more exact, the individual interest which the former sets out to protect is not the same as that protected by the latter. This may point to another reason why the combination of democracy and liberalism is possible but not essential.

No individualistic conception of society leaves out of account the fact that man is a social being, or considers the individual in isolation. Individualism is not to be confused with the kind of philosophical anarchism espoused by Stirner (1806–1856). However, liberalism and democracy differ in the way they understand the relation of the individual to society.

Liberalism amputates the individual from the organic body, makes him live – at least for much of his life – outside the maternal womb, plunges him into the unknown and perilous world of the struggle for survival. Democracy joins him together once more with others like himself, so that society can be built up again from their union, no longer as an organic whole but as an association of free individuals. Liberalism defends and proclaims individual liberty as against the state, in both the spiritual and the economic sphere; democracy reconciles individual and society by making society the product of a common agreement between individuals. For liberalism, the individual is the author of every kind of action performed outside the confines of the state; for democracy, he is the protagonist of a different kind of state, in which collective decisions are made directly by individuals or else by way of their delegates and representatives. Liberalism highlights the individual's capacity for self-creation, his ability to develop his own faculties and to progress intellectually and morally in conditions of maximum freedom from all externally and coercively imposed constraints; democracy holds in highest regard the individual's capacity to overcome isolation by devising various procedures allowing the institution of non-tyrranical common power. Of the two aspects of individuality, liberalism is concerned with what which is inward-looking, democracy with that which is outward-looking. Two different potential individuals are in question: the individual as microcosm or totality complete in itself, and the individual as a particle (or atom) which is indivisible, but which may be combined and recombined with other similar particles in various ways, giving rise to an artificial (and thus always fissionable) unity.

Both liberal individualism and democratic individualism come into being through the struggle against various modes of organicism, but by a process specific to each. For liberal individualism this takes the form of a gradual corrosion of the totality, akin to the manner in which children, on reaching the age of majority, detach themselves from the all-powerful and all-pervasive primitive group and conquer for themselves ever wider spheres of individual action. For democratic individualism on the other hand, it takes the form of an internal dissolution of the unified global compound, out of which are formed elements which are independent both of each other and of the whole, and are able thereupon to pursue a life of their own. The effect of the first process is to reduce public power to a minimum; of the second, to reconstitute it, but to reconstitute it as the sum of particular powers – as is plain in contract theory, which regards the state as founded upon a juridical institution, akin to the contract, and appertaining to the sphere of private rights, in which particular wills come together in the formation of a common will.

10

Liberals and Democrats in the Nineteenth Century

In Europe, the history of the liberal state and of its development into the democratic state can properly be said to have begun in the period of the restoration of the continental monarchies. Writing in the tenth year of the fascist regime (1932), Benedetto Croce (1866–1952) called this epoch (with a certain rhetorical emphasis understandable in the circumstances) the age of the 'religion of liberty', and claimed to perceive in it the 'germinal period' of a new civilization.[30] Croce's conception of liberty embraced liberty as understood by liberals (Croce speaks of 'the replacement of absolutism by constitutional government') as well as democratic liberty (electoral reform and a broadening of political participation), without clearly distinguishing between them; 'liberation from the dominion of foreigners', or liberty as national independence, is a further aspect. If we are looking for the 'germinal period', however, we must go further back in time – not indeed to the 'Germanic forests' in which Hegel, following Montesquieu, discerned the birthplace of modern liberty, but to the England of the seventeenth century, which saw the beginnings of the modern liberal state in theory and practice, and which for some centuries remained an ideal model for both Europe and the United States of America. It was the Puritan Revolution, with its ferment of ideas and religious sects and political movements, that opened the way for the advance of those ideas of liberty of the person, and of religious belief and freedom of opinion and of the press, which were destined to become the lasting heritage of liberal thought. Its bloody outcome sealed the supremacy of Parliament over the king, and led in time – gradually, and unevenly – to the establishment of the representative state as the ideal form of constitution, an ideal which still holds sway today (if only for lack of anything better to take its place); the doctrine of the separation of powers inspired Montesquieu, and through him American and European constitutionalism. If by democracy we mean, as in the present instance we do, the extension of political rights to all citizens above the age of majority, then the democratic ideal, too, was for the first time loudly proclaimed in the years of the 'great rebellion': it is in fact in the Levellers' 'Agreement of the People' (1648) that we first find challenged the ruling principle which debarred all non-landowners from political rights (and which was to remain in force for at least another two centuries), and supplanted by a proclamation of the democratic principles according to which

> The people of England ... for the election of their representatives, be more indifferently proportioned, and to this end, that the Representatives of the whole nations shall consist of 300 persons.... And in all elections ... they shall be men of one-and-twenty years old or upwards ...[31]

In England, moreover, and only in England, a peaceful and gradual process of evolution from within, unmarked by violent clashes or periods of reaction and regression, was to lead from the Glorious Revolution of 1688 to the replacement of constitutional by parliamentary monarchy and from a restricted to an enlarged democracy.

In France, which in many respects led the way for the

European continent, the process of democratization was a good deal more uneven. The 1848 revolution, which attempted to impose democracy by force, quickly collapsed, and led to the founding of a new regime of Caesarian stamp (Napoleon III's Second Empire). England's most recent Caesarian regime, the dictatorship of Cromwell, was already a distant event, but in France only a brief time elapsed between the Jacobin republic and the Napoleonic empire, a fact which stirred strongly liberal anti-democratic sentiments among the writers of the period: these proved longlasting, and profoundly influenced the debate as to whether the democratic state was a possible or desirable development of the liberal state. Conservative writers, in whose views we can detect echoes of classical thinkers and especially of Plato, almost unanimously agreed that democracy and tyranny were two sides of the same coin: Caesarian dictatorship was no more than the natural and terrible consequence of the disorders unleashed by the republic of demagogues. In the final pages of his *Democracy in America* Tocqueville (1805–1859) uttered his famous prophecy:

> I am trying to imagine under what novel features despotism may appear in the world. In the first place, I see an innumerable multitude of men, alike and equal, constantly circling around in pursuit of the petty and banal pleasures with which they glut their souls.... Over this kind of men stands an immense, protective power which is alone responsible for securing their enjoyment and watching over their fate.[32]

The still more rapid collapse of the ephemeral republic of 1848, and its replacement by the Second Empire, seemed to confirm the far-sighted investigator of American democracy in his forecast.

Throughout the century both liberalization and democratization continued to evolve, sometimes in tandem and sometimes separately, depending on whether the extension of the franchise was seen as an inherently necessary element of the liberal state or as an obstacle to its development which tended to the reduction rather than the enhancement of freedom. Differences of response to the issues raised by the relations between liberalism and democracy were reflected in a schism among the ranks of the liberals: on the one hand, there were the radical liberals, who were at once both liberal and democratic, and on the other the conservatives, who were not democrats and who ceaselessly contested every broadening of the franchise as a potential erosion of freedom. The democratic ranks were similarly riven by a confrontation between liberal and non-liberal democrats: the latter were concerned more with the distribution than with the limitations of power, more with instituting self-government than with the division of the central government's powers, more with the horizontal than with the vertical separation of powers, and more with the conquest of the public sphere than with the scrupulous defence of the private sphere. As the movement for the extension of political rights progressed through its more or less numerous and rapid stages towards the achievement of universal franchise, democratic liberals and liberal democrats gradually became more closely identified. The pure democrats were to find themselves standing alongside the earliest socialist movements, even if their relationship often involved mutual competition, as was the case in Italy with Mazzini's party. Between the pure democrats and the conservative liberals, the distance was such as to amount to mutual incompatibility.

The relations between liberalism and democracy can be schematically summarized in terms of three combinations: (a) liberalism and democracy are compatible, and can therefore coexist, in the sense that a state can exist which is at once both liberal and democratic: but this does not exclude the possibility of a liberal but non-democratic, or a democratic but non-liberal state (the former is envisaged by conservative liberals, the latter by radical democrats); (b) liberalism and democracy are antithetical in the sense that democracy pushed to its furthest limits ends in the destruction of the liberal state (this is the argument of the conservative liberals), or can only be fully realized in a social state that has abandoned the ideal of the minimal state (this is the argument of the radical democrats); (c) liberalism and democracy are necessarily interlinked in the sense that only democracy is able fully to realize the liberal ideal, and only in a liberal state can democracy be put into effect.

In formal terms, (a) involves a relation of possibility (liberalism *vel* democracy); (b) a relation of impossibility (liberalism *aut* democracy); (c) a relation of necessity (liberalism *et* democracy). From the moment that democracy as a form of government is associated equally with both liberalism and socialism, a similar framework can be employed to analyse the relations between democracy and socialism. These can be seen as involving possibility or possible coexistence, impossibility (this is the view of liberal democrats, and also at the opposite end of the spectrum, of those who advocate the dictatorship of the proletariat), or necessity, as maintained by the doctrines and movements of social democracy, in which democracy is regarded as the only means by which socialism can be realized, and socialism is regarded as the only way in which the process of democratization can be fully achieved.

11

The Tyranny of the Majority

The two wings of European liberalism, the one more conservative, the other more radical, are well represented respectively by Alexis de Tocqueville and by John Stuart Mill (1807–1873), the two major liberal writers of the last century. They were contemporaries (Tocqueville was born two years earlier than Mill) who both knew and admired each other. Mill wrote a long review of the first volume of *Democracy in America* for the *London Review*, the organ of the English radicals.[33] In his work on representative democracy, which appeared after Tocqueville's death (1861), Mill reminded his readers of his friend's 'great work'.[34] Tocqueville, for his part, wrote to Mill when he received the latter's essay on liberty (he himself was already dying at the time), that 'I feel certain of your continual awareness that where it is a case of exploring the terrain of liberty we have no choice but to proceed hand in hand'.[35] For all their differing traditions, cultures and temperaments, the works of these two authors well illustrate the communality of themes between the two chief traditions of European liberalism, the English and the French. Tocqueville had devoted years of study and reflection to the democracy of a new and forward-looking society, and Mill, less insular than many of his compatriots, was familiar with French thought, and first of all with that of Comte (1798–1857).

Tocqueville was a liberal before he was a democrat. He was firmly convinced that life in society must be based on and animated by liberty, above all religious and moral liberty (with economic liberty he was less concerned). He had realized, however, that the revolution had given birth to a century in headlong and unstoppable pursuit of democracy. Nothing could halt this process. In the introduction to the first part of his work (1835), he asked:

> Does anyone imagine that democracy, which has destroyed the feudal system and vanquished kings, will fall back before the middle classes and the rich? Will it stop now, when it has grown so strong and its adversaries so weak?[36]

His book, he explained, had been written under the impulse of a kind of religious awe provoked by the spectacle of the 'irresistible revolution', which overleaped all barriers and forged ahead even in the midst of the ruins that it had produced. Subsequent to his travels in America, where he had sought to understand the nature of the conditions of democratic society in a world very different from Europe, and where he had beheld 'democracy in its very image', he remained obsessed throughout the rest of his life with the question: 'Can liberty survive, and how can it survive, in a democratic society?'

For Tocqueville, 'democracy', under one of its aspects, means a form of government in which all participate in public affairs, and here it is the contrary of aristocracy; under another aspect, it denotes a society inspired by the ideal of equality, a society which will eventually come to overwhelm traditional social structures based on immutable hierarchies. For Tocqueville, as indeed for his friend Mill, democracy as a form of government brings in its train the danger of the tyranny of the majority: democracy as progressive realization of the egalitarian ideal is attended by the danger of levelling, which issues at length in despotism. These are two alternative forms of tyranny, and both of them, different though they are from one another, are the negation of liberty. The fact that Tocqueville nowhere in his work distinguishes properly between these two meanings of democracy may lead readers to arrive at divergent or even contradictory judgements as to his attitude to democracy. Where democracy is regarded not as a range of institutions whose touchstone is the institutionalized participation of the people in political power, but rather as an exaltation of the value of equality in a social as well as a political sense, or as the equalization of conditions without regard for liberty, Tocqueville shows himself to be a consistent liberal and not a democrat. He never hesitates for a moment in favouring individual liberty over social equality, whereas democratic peoples, he is convinced, even if they do have a natural inclination towards liberty, feel for equality a passion which is 'ardent, insatiable, eternal, and invincible'. Although 'they want equality in freedom', if they cannot have that, 'they still want equality in slavery'.[37] They will put up with poverty, but they will not endure aristocracy.

Chapter Seven of the first part of *Democracy in America* is devoted to a discussion of the tyranny of the majority. The principle that the majority should prevail is an egalitarian principle in that it advocates the prevalence of the force of numbers over that of a single individual; it rests upon the argument that 'there is more enlightenment and wisdom in a numerous assembly than in a single man, and the number of legislators is more important than how they are chosen. It is the theory of equality applied to brains'.[38]

When the majority is all-powerful, numerous ill effects ensue, among them the instability of the legislative body, the often arbitrary exercise of power by officials, conformity of opinion, and a dearth of men worthy of respect in the political domain. To a liberal of Tocqueville's stamp, power – whether it is the power of the monarch or of the people – is always an ill. The overriding political problem has to do not so much with who holds power as with the manner of its control and limitation. Government is to be adjudged good or bad not according to whether it is in the hands of the many or the few, but by how much or how little it is allowed to do.

> Omnipotence in itself seems a bad and dangerous thing.... So there is no power on earth in itself so worthy of respect or vested with such a sacred right that I would wish to let it act without control and dominate without obstacles. So when I see the right and capacity to do all given to any authority whatsoever, whether it be called people or king, democracy or aristocracy, and whether the scene of action is a monarchy or a republic, I say: the germ of tyranny is there, and I will go look for other laws under which to live.[39]

Tocqueville felt keenly that in the last instance the liberal ideal, which values above all personal independence in morals and sentiment, cannot be reconciled with the egalitarian ideal, which looks forward to a society whose members shall be as far as possible alike in their aspirations, tastes, needs and conditions of life. He never had much faith that liberty could survive in a democratic society, even if he was never able to resign himself to the idea that his contemporaries, and their future descendants, would be no more than contented slaves. In the memorable final pages of the second part of his 'great work' (published in 1840), he anticipates the moment when democracy will turn into its opposite, since it carries within itself the seeds of a new despotism in the form of a centralized and omnipresent government. Meditating on the classical notion of democracy which Constant so mistrusted, and on Rousseau's idea of the general will, he writes

> Our contemporaries ... conceive a government which is unitary, protective, and all-powerful, but elected by the people. Centralization is combined with the sovereignty of the people. That gives them a chance to relax. They console

themselves for being under schoolmasters by thinking that they have chosen them themselves.... Under this system the citizens quit their state of dependence just long enough to choose their masters and then fall back into it.[40]

Democracy, understood as the direct or indirect participation in political power of the people as a whole, is by no means a sufficient remedy in itself against society's decline into an ever less free condition: 'One should never expect', he exclaims towards the end of his discussion, 'a liberal, energetic, and wise government to originate in the votes of a people of servants'.[41] If there is a remedy – and Tocqueville never ceased to believe that there was, and indeed never ceased to suggest what it might be – it is to be sought first of all in the classical prescriptions of liberal tradition, and above all in the defence of certain individual liberties, such as freedom of the press and of association, and in general of all those individual rights which democratic states tend to disregard in the name of the collective interest; secondly, it is to be found in observance of those norms which at least guarantee equality before the law; and finally, in decentralization.

For the same reasons that he was a liberal before he was a democrat, Tocqueville was never drawn to socialism; on the contrary, he frequently expressed his profound aversion to it. One can be simultaneously both liberal and democrat or both democrat and socialist; to be simultaneously both liberal and socialist is rather harder. When it came to the underlying confrontation between democracy and the lofty ideal of liberty, Tocqueville was not a democrat, but he became a defender of democracy where it was a case of countering socialism, which he saw as the manifestation of the collective state aimed at the creation of a society of beavers rather than of men. On 12 September 1848, he made a speech in the Constituent Assembly on the right to work, in the course of which he recalled and praised American democracy: it was completely immune, he declared, from the danger of socialist infection. Democracy and socialism, he went on, are by no means akin: 'they are not different, but opposed'. They have just one word in common: equality. 'But mark the difference', he concludes, 'democracy wants equality in the degree of liberty enjoyed by all, socialism in the degree of interference and slavery'.[42]

12

Liberalism and Utilitarianism

Mill, unlike Tocqueville, was both a liberal and a democrat. He regarded democracy, and especially representative government (which he also called 'popular' government), as the natural development and consequence of liberal principles. He recognized, to be sure, the ills to which democratic government was subject. But in seeking to remedy those ills, he displayed greater faith in the future, looking forward to gradual and inevitable progress. In his later writings, he even adopted the view that liberalism and socialism are not incompatible. His two chief works of political theory (Mill was primarily a philosopher and economist) were *On Liberty* (1859) and *Representative Government* (1863). While Tocqueville was a historian and political writer, Mill was additionally a political theorist, and was endowed far more than his French admirer with the talents and temperament of the reformer.

Mill's great teacher in matters of theory was Jeremy Bentham (1748–1832), whose utilitarian philosophy provided Mill with a new foundation for liberal argument unlike any found in previous writers. So it was that Mill originated, or rather lent his significant authority, to what was subsequently to establish itself as by far the most important current of liberalism. Earlier doctrines had based the argument that governments had a duty to restrict the exercise of public power on the existence of the individual's natural, and therefore inviolable, rights. Bentham, in his essay on 'Anarchical Fallacies' of 1795, had launched a violent attack on the French Declarations of Rights, pillorying them with disdainful irony for their philosophical feebleness, logical incoherence, verbal equivocation and utter lack of practical effect. The declaration proclaiming that all men are born free he dismissed as absurd and utter foolishness, claiming that there was no such thing as natural rights, or rights prior to the institution of government, or rights opposed to or in contradiction with those of law.[43] In place of the long-established natural rights tradition, Bentham set up the 'principle of utility', according to which the only criterion that should inspire a good legislator was that the greatest happiness of the greatest number should be promoted by the laws. This meant that any such limits as might be placed on the power of those who govern had nothing to do with fantasies about natural rights, which do not exist and cannot possibly be proved to exist, but follow from the objective consideration that men seek pleasure and avoid pain, and that the best society is therefore the society which succeeds in obtaining the greatest happiness for the greatest number of its members. In the Anglo-Saxon intellectual tradition, which has undoubtedly made the most enduring and coherent contribution to the development of liberalism, utilitarianism and liberalism were to proceed in parallel from the time of Bentham onwards, with utilitarianism becoming the major theoretical ally of the liberal state. In moving from the doctrine of natural rights to utilitarianism, liberal thought underwent a fundamental crisis, whose effects are still traceable in the recently renewed debate around the issue of human rights.

Mill is an explicit and convinced utilitarian:

> The creed which accepts as the foundation of morals, Utility, or the Greatest Happiness Principle, holds that actions are right in proportion as they tend to promote happiness, wrong as they tend to produce the reverse of happiness.[44]

He interpreted Bentham's 'happiness' as equivalent to pleasure or the absence of pain, and his 'unhappiness' as pain or the loss of pleasure. As a moral doctrine, however, and a doctrine which criticizes and rejects any form of fundamental moral obligation unless it refers back to the question of pain and pleasure, utilitarianism, Mill argued, is concerned not with utility as it applies to the isolated individual in his relation to the utility of other such individuals, but with social utility; not with 'the agent's own happiness, but that of all concerned', a matter to be assessed with the impartiality of a 'disinterested and benevolent spectator'.[45] Mill accordingly rejects the temptation to fall back on the doctrine of natural rights as foundation and vindication of the notion that state power must be limited (and in this his position is consistent with Bentham's critique of natural rights). He makes this point expressly in his introduction to *On Liberty*, where he sets out the principles which inspire his doctrines:

> It is proper to state that I forgo any advantage which could be derived to my argument from the idea of abstract right, as a thing dependent on utility. I regard utility as the ultimate appeal on all ethical questions; but it must be utility in the largest sense, grounded on the permanent interests of man as a progressive being.[46]

Mill follows liberal tradition in concerning himself with negative liberty, liberty understood as the condition of a subject (whether an individual or a group acting as a single whole) not hindered by any external force from doing what it desires and not under any compulsion to do what it does not desire. Mill is thus seeking to formulate a principle on which he can base and establish, on the one hand, the limits within which public power can legitimately restrict the liberty of individuals; on the other hand, and as a corollary, the limits within which individuals or groups can act without the interference of state power. In other words, he is seeking to draw the boundary between private and public spheres in such a way as to guarantee individual enjoyment of a liberty unmarred by the incursion of state power, and to ensure that the margins of this liberty will be as wide as is consistent with making the necessary allowance for mediation between individual and collective interests. The principle he proposes is as follows:

> That the sole end for which mankind are warranted, individually or collectively, in interfering with the liberty of action of any of their number, is self-protection. That the only purpose for which power can be rightfully exercised over any member of a civilized community, against his will, is to prevent harm to others.[47]

From which it follows in turn that 'If any one does an act hurtful to others, there is a *prima facie* case for punishing him, by law, or, where legal penalties are not safely applicable, by general disapprobation'.[48]

In enunciating this principle, Mill aims to limit the state's right to restrict the sphere of individual liberty – the sphere where the individual is free to choose between alternatives; and to limit its rights to induce citizens to act or refrain from acting, other than in accordance with their own wishes, to the realm of external actions (in Kant's sense). The state, in other words, can legitimately interfere only in the case of those actions in which the individual's pursuit of his own interests may infringe upon the interests of another individual. It follows that the individual is protected from any incursion of public power so long as his actions affect nobody but himself – for instance, in his private thoughts and feelings, his liberty of thought and opinion, his freedom to follow his own tastes and projects, his freedom to associate with other individuals. If we agree to call 'paternalistic' all those political doctrines which regard the state as entitled to interfere in individuals' private affairs on the grounds that every individual, even an adult, requires protection against his own inclinations and impulses, then here in Mill, as in Locke and Kant, liberalism once again shows itself to be the anti-paternalistic doctrine *par excellence*; for its starting-point is the ethical premise forcefully expressed in the Millian dictum that each individual 'is the proper guardian of his own health, whether bodily, *or* mental and spiritual'.[49] This is not to deny that elements of paternalism are to be found in Mill (as they are in Locke and Kant, come to that). We have here in mind the fact that Mill, in expressing the opinion just cited, restricts its application to the members of a 'civilized community': the principle of liberty, in other words, holds good only for individuals whose faculties are fully developed. It does not hold good for minors, who are still under paternal protection, or for backward societies, which can be considered as being in a condition of collective minority. Mill makes his opinion on the latter point quite clear: 'Despotism is a legitimate mode of government in dealing with barbarians, provided the end be their improvement, and the means justified by actually effecting that end'.[50] Leaving aside the qualifying clause (though who is to be the judge of the end pursued or of the appropriateness of the means to that end?), Mill here echoes faithfully the traditional justification for despotic regimes, which Aristotle, centuries earlier, had thought the right form of government for those who were by nature slaves.

13

Representative Democracy

Mill, like Tocqueville, fears the tyranny of the majority and regards it as one of the evils against which society must protect itself. However, this does not lead him to reject democratic government. In his work on representative democracy, written shortly after *On Liberty*, he asks himself the time-honoured question, What is the best form of government? and concludes that it is, in fact, representative democracy, which constitutes, at any rate in those nations that have advanced to a certain level of civilization, the natural development of any state seeking to guarantee the maximum freedom for its citizens: 'the participation of all in these benefits is the ideally perfect conception of free government'. And he supports the claim with the following observation:

> In proportion as any, no matter who, are excluded from it, the interests of the excluded are left without the guarantee accorded to the rest, and they themselves have less scope and encouragement than they might otherwise have to that exertion of their energies for the good of themselves and of the community.[51]

Here we find the clearest possible expression of the link between liberalism and democracy or, more precisely, between a particular conception of the state, and those modes and forms of the exercise of power that are best fitted to realize this conception in actuality.

This view that the perfectly free government is that in which all participate, to the benefit of all, led Mill to become an advocate of the extension of the franchise. Here he followed Benthamite radicalism, which had pressed for the English electoral reform of 1832. One remedy against the tyranny of the majority lies in extending participation at elections beyond the leisured classes (always a minority of the population and naturally showing a tendency to be exclusively concerned with their own interests), so allowing the majority to include the popular classes provided that they are tax-payers on however small a scale. Voting has great educational value: political discussion encourages the manual labourer, despite the repetitive character of his work and the narrow horizons of the factory, to arrive at some understanding of the relation between distant events and his own personal interests and to establish relations with citizens unlike those with whom he is in daily intercourse at work. He thus becomes a conscious member of a great community: 'There ought to be no pariahs in a full-grown and civilized nation; no persons disqualified, except through their own default'.[52]

Universal suffrage nonetheless remains ideal, an ultimate objective, and Mill's own proposals fall considerably short of it: Mill excludes from the vote not only bankrupts and fraudulent debtors, but also the illiterate (though he looks forward to universal education, which, he says, must precede universal suffrage) and those in receipt of parish relief, for he holds that those who make no contribution at all by way of taxes can have no right to decide how everyone is to contribute to public expenditure. On the other hand, Mill supports the enfranchisement of women (whereas in continental Europe the vote was generally extended to illiterate men earlier than to women), basing his position on the argument that all human beings have an interest in being well governed and that each person thus has an equal need of the vote in order to ensure his or her rightful share of the benefits accruing to each member of the community. This leads him to turn on its head the usual anti-feminist argument: if there is any difference of claim, says Mill, 'women require it more than men, since, being physically weaker, they are more dependent on law and society for protection'.[53]

Mill's second remedy against the tyranny of the majority is reform of the electoral system. He advocates a change from the majority vote system – whereby each constituency is allowed to elect no more than one representative, the successful candidate being the one to receive the most votes (whether in one or more rounds) and the rest being eliminated – in favour of a proportional system (Mill's model was that proposed by Thomas Hare, 1806–1891); such a system ensures that minorities will be adequately represented, each in proportion to the votes it receives, and may be based either on a single nationwide constituency, or on constituencies large enough to allow the election of several representatives. Outlining the advantages and merits of the scheme, Mill emphasizes that the majority will be held in check by the presence of a diehard minority, who will hinder any abuse of power which might otherwise be open to it, and who will thus prevent democracy from degenerating. He takes this opportunity to pen one of the most forceful eulogies of antagonism to be found in liberal thought, in a passage offering what is surely a quintessential expression of the liberal ethic:

No community has ever long continued progressive, but while a conflict was going on between the strongest power in the community and some rival power; between the spiritual and temporal authorities; the military or territorial and the industrious classes; the king and the people; the orthodox and the religious reformers.[54]

Wherever conflict is stifled or smoothed away, stagnation invariably sets in, followed by the decline and decay of the state or of an entire civilization.

Although Mill fully accepts the democratic principle, and although he praises representative democracy as the best form of government, his thought still falls far short of embracing the ideal of perfect democracy. As if to modify the innovatory effects of a wider franchise, he proposed the institution of plural votes (a proposal that was not taken up): although it is only just that everyone should have the vote, it does not follow from this, he argues, that each elector is entitled to just one vote. The best educated, Mill proposes (and not those who are wealthiest), should have more than one vote, adding the proviso that those who apply for them and succeed in passing an examination should also be entitled to extra votes. Modern constitutions however affirm, not without reason, that the right to vote should be an 'equal' right (as stated in Article Forty-eight of the present Italian constitution).

14

Liberalism and Democracy in Italy

Even though its liberalism retained strongly paternalistic elements and rested on an incomplete and inegalitarian model of democracy, Mill's work represented a fruitful encounter between liberal and democratic thought. Nonetheless, liberals and democrats continued, as they do to this day, to organize themselves into different political movements and factions. At times, these will be directly opposed, as is the case when the liberals, for their part, direct their polemic at the growing incursions of the state, which they rightly interpret as a consequence of democratization; or the democrats for their part challenge the continuation of political oligarchies and marked economic inequalities, which they rightly claim are a consequence of the slow pace at which democratization is proceeding and of the obstacles put in its path by those blessed by wealth. The opposition between liberalism and democracy in this area can also be considered from another point of view: there is a close connection between the development of liberal doctrine and the economic critique of autocratic societies, whereas the development of democratic doctrine tends rather to be associated with a political or institutional critique. At all events, liberalism and democracy designated mutually antagonistic doctrines and movements throughout the last century.

Liberals supported the moves towards establishing or claiming rights and liberties which were associated with the period of the restoration, and were suspicious of the democrats' nostalgia for the age of revolution. Democrats, holding that the restoration had brought to a premature halt the process of popular emancipation initiated in the French revolution, dismissed the liberals as the party of moderation. Until the advent of the socialist parties, parliamentarians were divided between the party of conservatism and the party of progress, these two opposing formations corresponding more or less to the opposition between liberals and democrats. The dialectic of politics is best understood as alternating between these camps, even though in England, homeland of parliamentarianism and two-party government, they referred to themselves respectively as conservatives and liberals (the names were retained despite changes over time in their programmes). The disposing factors in the gradual confluence of the liberal and democratic traditions were, in the first instance, the formation of the socialist parties, and even more importantly, in the present century, the establishment of regimes that were neither liberal nor democratic – the fascist regimes and the regime that came to power as a result of the Russian October Revolution. The original differences between liberalism and democracy dwindled into historical and political irrelevance in the face of the new phenomenon of twentieth-century totalitarianism.

Italian political thought in the second half of the nineteenth century (which follows the broad lines of European, and in particular French, political thought) reveals a very clear opposition between liberal and democratic schools of thought. This was highlighted through the presence on the Italian scene of Mazzini (1805–1872), active as a writer and political agitator, and known beyond his native land as one of the most typical exponents of the new democratic ideas which were putting all Europe in a ferment as the old autocracies were challenged.

In the course of his account of Mazzini's literary work, Francesco De Sanctis (1817–1883) outlined and emphasized the distinction between liberal and democratic doctrines. These, he argued, were the two currents that animated the public mind of Italy in the nineteenth century; and although concerned above all with their literary aspect, he stressed their similarity in bringing together political, moral and religious objectives, with the result that, unlike the purely literary groups, they affected Italian society as a whole and not merely the narrow circle of the literary intelligentsia. De Sanctis, moreover, in the course of his discussion on Mazzini, applauded his role in the furtherance of national education through the stimulus he gave to the formation of a left-wing youth movement dedicated to re-directing the country along new lines and to promoting 'a new attitude towards the popular classes, a new concept of what is national – different from that which the right has traditionally upheld, because broader, less elitist and less authoritarian'.[55] He took the view that the liberal school had abandoned the goal of ultimate liberty proclaimed by the philosopher-revolutionaries of the seventeenth century, and had settled for liberty in a purely 'procedural' sense, as the method or means of a merely formal liberty, which anyone was entitled to avail themselves of in pursuit of their own private ends. The liberal school, he observed, was a sort of common ground

> open to men pursuing the most divergent ends. Here we find clerics anxious to preserve the freedom of the Church, conservatives seeking the liberty of the upper classes, democrats seeking the liberty of the lower, the friends of progress in search of a way forward without disturbing nature's modest pace of change.[56]

The democratic school, by contrast, argued De Sanctis, was inspired by the ideal of a new society 'based on distributive justice, and on equality of rights – which means, in the most

advanced countries, equality in reality also'. For the democrats, liberty was not a procedure but something 'substantial'.[57] Expanding on this point, he wrote:

> Where inequality prevails, liberty may be proclaimed in laws
> and statutes, but it does not really exist. There is no liberty for
> the peasant who depends on the landowner, the supplicant
> who asks a favour of the boss, or the serf condemned to
> ceaseless toil in the fields.[58]

Ideas such as these, concluded De Sanctis, could only lead
to the *res publica*, which is 'not the government of this or that
person, nor arbitrary power, nor the dominion of certain
classes: it is the government of all'.[59] A state for which liberty is
no more than a means can be neutral, indifferent, atheistic.
The state which belongs to all, the *res publica*, can be none of
these things; on the contrary, it must aim at educating the
nation, especially in the aftermath of a rapid and forced
process of unification.

Still in the Italian context, a nice instance of this persistent
opposition, as it appeared during the Risorgimento, is
presented by the contrasting figures of Cavour (1810–1868)
and Mazzini. From his youthful reading of Bentham, together
with Constant, Cavour retained principles to which he
remained faithful thereafter. From Bentham he took the idea
that the theory of natural rights lacked any foundation, and he
was also strongly convinced of the excellence of utilitarianism,
so much so that he was happy to regard himself as a 'hardened
Benthamite'.[60] In *I sistemi e la democrazia. Pensieri* (1850), one of
the fullest expressions of his doctrine, Mazzini argued that
Bentham and his utilitarian doctrines should be regarded as
the prime source of the materialism that held sway in democratic and socialist thought from Saint-Simon (1760–1825)
through the communists (among whom, however, he
mentions by name neither Marx (1818–1883) nor Engels
(1820–1895)); Bentham, he says, is the 'principal figure of this

school and the architect of its principles',[61] and his disciples include all those who 'worship utility'. In the place of the doctrine of utility, Mazzini puts forward the notion of duty and sacrifice in the name of the sacred cause of humanity:

> No, it is not by way of interest and pleasure that democracy finds means to improve the life of society; theoretical consider-ations of utility are not going to make the wealthy in all their ease feel the wretchedness of the poor and the urgent necessity of some remedy.[62]

Cavour was an admirer of Tocqueville and shared his anxiety about humanity's inexorable progress towards demo-cracy. It was Tocqueville who, as foreign minister of the French republic from June 1849 onwards, sealed the fate of the Roman republic. Mazzini addressed a vehement letter of protest to him and his fellow minister, Falloux (1811–1886), accusing the two of being the 'latest recruits to that school which began by spreading atheistical doctrines about art and has ended up pursuing power for power's sake'.[63] Cavour, advocate of the golden mean, sought an intermediate position, the only one conforming to reason, between reaction and revolution. Mazzini remained intransigent in his commitment to the national revolution, and associated himself unequivo-cally with one of the two extremes rejected by the liberal advocates of flexibility, Cavour was a student of economics and admirer of the great economists from Smith to Ricardo (1772–1823); he was a convinced and adamant believer in laissez-faire and the free trade theory, to which Mazzini remained steadfastly opposed. Mazzini proclaimed the edu-cational role and responsibility of the state, in opposition to the liberal view of it as a necessary evil whose functions should accordingly be restricted to the policing of society. Nothing could be more foreign to the opinions of a thoroughgoing liberal like Cavour than Mazzini's assault upon the idea that the state should be 'bereft of any powers to initiate, and function in a purely restraining capacity': the result, says Mazzini, is that

> in place of society, we have a mass of separate individuals, shackled and rendered passive, but all pursuing their own particular ends and all free to choose their own manner of life whether or not it is advantageous to the common cause. In politics as in economics, the great formula of this school of thought is *laissez faire, laissez passer.*[64]

Cavour, with his gradualist faith in the progressive adaptation of institutions to the changing needs of society, can have had little stomach for the abstract revolutionarism of Mazzini, for whom the simple, sane criterion of utility was supplanted by the imperative of sacrifice, and who transformed the stress on individual rights associated with the Enlightenment into a strict code of duty. Romeo states that 'Cavour, faithful to his Benthamite origins, held the view that economic progress, far from conflicting with spiritual and moral progress, in fact runs parallel to it.'[65] Mazzini, loyal to his anti-Benthamite origins, argues, by contrast, that spiritual progress is the condition of material progress: doctrines of happiness and well-being drawn from the utilitarian school make for an egoistic cult of materialism. 'What is needed, therefore, is a higher educative principle ... the principle of duty.'[66]

15

Democracy as It Relates to Socialism

Although liberal and democratic ideals have gradually fused in the course of their troubled history, the opposition between liberalism and democracy remains as strong as ever, and may even in recent years be said to have grown more acute in certain respects.

It is an opposition kept alive and intensified by a fact that supervened during the second half of the last century: the entry into the political arena of the workers' movement, which increasingly drew its inspiration from socialist doctrines. These latter were antithetical to those of liberalism, although the democratic method was not rejected – not, at any rate, by a large part of the movement, which included the English Labour Party, the German Social Democrats, and the reformist wing generally. As we have seen, liberalism and democracy have never been radically antithetical, even though it proved difficult and contentious to graft democratic ideals on to the original stock of liberal aspirations, and even though where liberalism and democracy have come together the process has been slow, painful and uneven. Socialism, on the other hand, clearly appeared as opposed to liberalism from the beginning – and not merely in its Marxist or *marxisant* guise. The bone of contention was economic liberty, which presupposes an unyielding commitment to private property. Despite the many different definitions which have been given of socialism over the last century, there is one criterion which consistently, distinctively and definitely marks it off from other doctrines: namely, the critique of private property as the principal source of 'inequalities among men' (to use the words of Rousseau's celebrated *Discourse*), and the view that the total or partial elimination of private property was the goal of the society of the future. Most socialist writers, and most of the movements they have inspired, have identified liberalism (rightly or wrongly – though certainly rightly in purely historical terms) with a commitment to defend economic freedom and thus individual property as its sole guarantee, this being regarded as a form of freedom essential to the flourishing of any other forms. The socialist movement inherited from bourgeois theories of history a class-based conception of history, according to which classes are the leading historical subjects and historical development comes about through the transition from the rule of one class to that of another. In this conception, liberalism, understood as the view that economic liberty is the foundation of all other liberties and that no man can be truly free in its absence, came in the end to be regarded by socialist writers (and not only by Marx, though it was Marx's influence that predominated in the formation of the continental socialist parties, especially in Germany and Italy) as nothing more than the ideology of the bourgeois class – the ideology, in other words, of the opposing party with which the socialists would have to do battle until they were finally eliminated.

While the relation between liberalism and socialism was one of clear antithesis (whether the criterion was socialism's project for the future society or its status as the ideology of a class destined, in the course of historical progress, to take the place of the bourgeoisie), the relation between socialism and democracy was complementary, like that which had hitherto held between democracy and liberalism. Though reckoned incompatible with liberalism, socialism gradually came to be thought of as congruent with democracy. Two arguments were advanced in support of this conception of their compatible, even complementary status. In the first place, it was claimed that as democratization proceeded so it would inevitably lead to, or at any rate foster, the advent of a socialist society, based on the transformation of the institution of private property and on the collectivization of at least the principal means of production. Secondly, it was argued that only by way of the advent of socialism could participation in political life be strengthened and enlarged, and democracy fully realized. Among the promises held out by such a democracy, moreover, was that of an equal (or at any rate more equal) distribution not only of political but of economic power, and this was something that a merely liberal democracy could never have offered. These two theses were the basis of the claim that democracy and socialism were indissolubly linked: the main strands of the socialist movement saw this link as a necessary condition for the creation of a socialist society, while democratic movements saw it as a condition of the development of democracy itself.

This is not to suggest that the relationship between democracy and socialism was always peaceful. Indeed, it mirrored that between liberalism and democracy in being, around certain issues, quite frequently and openly contestatory. Democracy and socialism, it was clear, reinforced one another in a circular relation; from which point on this circle should one attempt to initiate change? To begin by widening the scope of democracy implied the acceptance of a gradual and uncertain process of development. Was it possible, desirable and legitimate to take the opposite approach – to set out at once on the path of socialist transformation of society, by way of a qualitative, revolutionary break which would involve at least a temporary suspension of the methods of democracy? Thus it was that from the second half of the last century onwards, the conflict between liberalism and democracy was overlaid by a new opposition between the defenders of liberal democracy, on the one hand, who often formed common cause against socialism (which they regarded as the negation of both liberalism and democracy) and, on the other hand, the socialists, both democratic and non-democratic. These in turn were divided not over their attitude to liberalism, which they agreed in opposing, but by their judgement of the validity and efficacy of democracy, at least in the immediate aftermath of the conquest of power. However, such doubts about the appropriateness of democratic methods during the so-called transition period never in any way negated the fundamental democratic inspiration of the socialist parties, based as this was on a conviction that democracy would best be advanced in a socialist society and that the latter would prove in the long run more democratic than a liberal society which has sprung up and been nurtured along with the birth and growth of capitalism.

Surveying the vast literature of the past century, we can identify at least three arguments advanced in support of this view that socialist democracy is preferable to liberal democracy: (a) Liberal democracy – or, in more polemical terms, capitalist democracy and (with regard to the historical subject which brought it into being) bourgeois democracy – came into existence as representative democracy, with elected representatives unfettered by any mandate; while socialist or, in class terms, proletarian democracy is to be a direct democracy, in the double sense either of a democracy of all the people without representatives or else of a democracy based, not on representatives, but on mandated delegates subject to recall. (b) Bourgeois democracy has allowed people to participate in political power, both central and local, through the extension of the suffrage to the point where all men and women enjoy the vote; but only socialist democracy will allow them to participate also in decisions on economic matters, which in capitalist society are taken autocratically. In this sense, socialist democracy represents not just a more active participation, but a quantitative extension of participation through the opening up of new spaces for the exercise of that popular sovereignty which constitutes the essence of democracy. (c) Finally, and above all, liberal democracy offers the right to participate directly or indirectly in political decisions, but this is not paralleled by any increased equality in the distribution of economic power, with the result that the right to vote often amounts to nothing more than a mirage. Socialist democracy, by contrast, holds a more equal distribution of economic power to be one of the prime aims of the changes which it aims to institute in the economic regime, and thus transforms the formal power to participate into a real and substantial power, at the same time bringing democracy itself to its ideal fulfilment, a greater equality among men.

The fact that the democratic ideal has been embraced by both the liberal movement and by the antithetical socialist movement, with the result that both liberal-democratic and social-democratic governments have come into being (though as yet no socialist-democratic government; we have yet to see a regime which is both democratic and socialist), might incline one to conclude that for the last two centuries democracy has figured as a kind of common denominator among all the regimes that have developed in the economically and politically advanced countries. However, we should not automatically assume that the concept of democracy has remained unaltered in the passage from liberal to social democracy. In the liberalism–democracy couple, democracy means above all universal suffrage, and thus a means whereby particular individuals can freely express their will. In the socialism–democracy coupling, it signifies above all the egalitarian ideal, which can only be achieved by the property reforms proposed by socialism. In the former case democracy is a consequence, in the latter it is a presupposition. As a consequence, it is the political liberty which follows from and completes the series of more particular liberties; as a presupposition, it remains to be completed, and can only be completed under the changed conditions which socialism aspires to create through the transformation of capitalist society.

The ambiguous nature of the concept of democracy is very manifest in the so-called 'social democracy', which has been the architect of the 'welfare state'.* Social democracy claims to represent an advance on liberal democracy in that its declaration of rights embraces social rights as well as rights to liberty; with respect to socialist democracy, on the other hand, it claims only to be a first phase. The ambiguity has been reflected in the double-edged nature of the critique which it has elicited, with intransigent liberals on the right claiming that it diminishes the liberty of the individual, while on the left, impatient socialists condemn it as a compromise between old and new which, far from favouring the realization of socialism, hinders or renders it altogether inoperable.

---

* Bobbio uses the Italian term *stato dei servizi* (literally 'service state'), explaining that he prefers it to the other terms in use in Italy: *stato benessere* ('welfare state') and *stato assistenziale* ('assistance state'), which he claims err respectively by overstating or understating the blessings of such a state. [Trans.]

16

The New Liberalism

Let us now return to our theme: the relationship between liberalism and democracy. There is no doubt that the emergence and spread of socialist doctrines and movements, and the accompanying explicit alliance between the latter and democratic parties, reopened the longstanding conflict between liberalism and democracy – and at the very moment, too, when the progress of the most advanced countries towards universal suffrage was promising a final historic reconciliation between the two. If – as the social democratic parties claimed in the programme of the Second International – the process of progressive democratization was bound inevitably to lead to socialism, then could it be supported by liberals? It was precisely in reaction to this supposed advance of socialism, with its general programme of economic planning and collectivization of the means of production, that liberal argument has come to focus ever more narrowly on the defence of the market economy and of freedom of enterprise (together with the connected right to private property), and has become identified with the economic position known in Italian politics as *liberismo*. As always happens, and despite the fact that liberalism and socialism are mutually opposed ideologies both in their origins and in their programmatic outlines, attempts have been made to overcome their antithesis by way of mediation or synthesis: these have ranged from the well-known *Liberalism* (1911) of Hobhouse (1864–1929) to the *Socialismo Liberale* (1930) of Carlo Roselli (1899–1937), and the liberal socialism, which also attracted its advocates in Italy (but was a formula unknown elsewhere), and which inspired the small anti-Fascist *Partito d'Azione* during its brief period of activity (1942–1947). However, the antithesis has persisted, and indeed become even more rigid and sharply defined in the course of the last two decades. There are two very obvious historical reasons for this. In the first place, the flagrantly illiberal nature of those regimes which have attempted, for the first time, to transform society along socialist lines; in the second, the emergence of illiberal elements in the policies of those governments which have gone furthest in implementing the welfare state. Liberal socialism (or liberal-socialism) has hitherto remained either an abstract doctrinal idea, as tempting in theory as it is hard to translate into institutional practice, or else a formula (by no means the only one) of use in designating those forms of government wherein the state apparatus is deployed in the protection of social as well as liberal rights.

If, then, a marriage between liberalism and socialism has hitherto been a vain, if worthy aspiration, there is no denying the very real nature of the increasing identification of liberalism with the defence of the free market. There can be no proper understanding of one of the most important aspects of the current political struggles of western Europe and the United States if one fails to take note of this reality. In Italy, the nature of the issues was made particularly clear in the debate between Croce and Einaudi (1874–1961), which took place during the last years of the fascist regime, and centred on the relationship between ethical–political liberalism and economic liberalism. Einaudi, as a liberal economist, maintained that there was an indissoluble connection between the ethical–political doctrine and economic liberalism (or the defence of the free market), and that without the latter, the former could not survive. Croce, though in certain respects more of a conservative than Einaudi, opposed this view and argued that liberty was a moral ideal and as such could be realized in a range of economic dispensations, provided these were directed to the moral improvement of the individual; and he cited with approval Hobhouse's 'fine eulogy and apologia' for liberal socialism.[67]

If we consider the current meaning of the term liberalism, especially in the usage of the various so-called neo-liberal currents of thought, then we must conclude that the economist, Einaudi, has been proved right. Neo-liberalism today refers primarily to a widely supported economic doctrine, while political liberalism is regarded as no more than a means (and not even always a necessary means) to its realization; or else it represents an uncompromising commitment to an economic liberty of which political freedom is viewed as no more than a corollary. The Austrian economist, Friedrich von Hayek, one of the key influences behind the present moves to dismantle the welfare state, has been as insistent as anyone on the indissolubility of the connection between economic liberty and liberty *tout court*. He has in consequence stressed the importance of clearly distinguishing between liberalism, whose starting-point is in economic theory; and democracy, which is a political theory. For Hayek, individual liberty, of which the first condition is economic freedom, possesses intrinsic value, whereas democracy's value is only instrumental. He grants that liberalism and democracy may have stood side by side, and even been confused with one another, in the old struggles against absolutism, but the time for such confusion is past now that it has been brought home to us (not least through the illiberalism to which the process of democratization is potentially – and indeed actually – subject) that the two doctrines are responses to different problems. Liberalism is concerned with the problem of governmental functioning, and in particular with limiting the powers of government, while democracy is concerned with the problem of who is to govern and by what procedures:

> Liberalism requires that all power, and this must include the power of the majority, must be circumscribed. Democracy, by contrast, tends to the view that the opinion of the majority constitutes the sole limit to the powers of the government. The difference between the two principles is clearly apparent when we recall that the opposite of democracy is authoritarianism, and the opposite of liberty, totalitarianism.[68]

Of course, the term 'liberalism', like every other term of political discourse, has had various meanings which have enjoyed more or less wide currency. Nonetheless Hayek's views, expressed in a considerable number of works which may well be regarded as the epitome of contemporary liberal thinking, are an authoritative confirmation of the original kernel of classical liberalism as a theory of the limits of state power, premised upon the individual as possessor, prior to the emergence of political power, of certain interests and rights, including the right to private property. These limits apply to whoever holds political power, extending even to the case of popular power or in other words of democratic government, where all citizens have the right to participate, even if only indirectly, in the making of important decisions, and which is subject to the rule of the majority. It is impossible to demarcate once and for all the boundary between the powers of the state and the rights of the individual: nonetheless, liberal doctrine in all its traditional expressions, and especially in the Anglo-Saxon world, has characteristically and repeatedly taken the view that those states are most liberal which wield the least power, and in which, as a corollary, the sphere of negative liberty is widest. Liberalism differs from authoritarianism (which is nonetheless regarded as preferable to totalitarianism) in its valuation of the two antithetical terms, power and liberty, and of their respective consequences. For liberalism, the positive sign is attached to the term 'liberty', and those societies are accordingly deemed best where liberty is at its widest and power at its most restricted.

Liberalism is today often defined as the doctrine of the 'minimal state'. Whereas the anarchist regards the state as an absolute evil, which must therefore be done away with, the liberal regards it as evil but also as necessary, and hence as indispensable, although it should never be extended beyond the absolute minimum. The great attention paid to this notion of the 'minimal state' explains why there has been such a wealth of discussion centred on Robert Nozick's book, *Anarchy, State and Utopia*, which appeared in 1974.[69] Nozick directs his attack at two targets: at the maximal state advocated by those who believe in 'the just state' (whose tasks would include the redistribution of wealth); and also at anarchist proposals that the state should be completely eliminated. Though he deploys some fresh arguments, Nozick offers a restatement and a defence of the classic liberal thesis that the state is an organization enjoying the exclusive right to the use of force and entrusted with the single, limited task of protecting the individual rights of each member of the group. His starting-point is Locke's theory of the state of nature and of natural rights, even though he rejects contract theory with its view of the state as arising from a voluntary agreement, preferring the convenient (and perhaps mistaken) notion that it is the creation of an 'invisible hand'. The state, he argues, is a free association into which those who live in a given territory enter for the sake of protection, and its task is to defend the rights of each individual against interference on the part of any other, and accordingly to prevent the development of any form of private protection, or in other words, to stop individuals meting out their own private justice. When he turns to the question of which individual rights the state should protect, Nozick bases his theory on a number of general principles of private right, which lay down that individuals have a right to possess what they have justly acquired (the principle of justice in acquisition), including whatever they have justly acquired from a previous owner (the principle of justice in transfer). If the state takes on any tasks beyond these, it acts unjustly in that it interferes unduly in the lives and liberties of individuals. The minimal state, Nozick concludes, may be minimal, but it is the only state properly speaking that we can conceive of: anything more extended in scope is immoral.

Nozick's theory raises more problems than it solves. It depends entirely on our acceptance of the juridical doctrine concerning acquired and derived entitlement to property, which Nozick altogether fails to discuss. For all that, it is an excellent illustration of the lengths to which the authentic liberal tradition can go in its defence of the minimal state as against the welfare conception which envisages social justice as falling within the purview of the state. And as such, it inevitably has an account to settle with the tradition of democratic thought; not so much in respect of egalitarian democracy (for as we have said all along this is difficult to reconcile with the spirit of liberalism), but rather in regard to the very forms of democracy. For wherever those forms have been put into effect – even in countries such as the United States, where no socialist party has emerged – the result has been a degree of state intervention incompatible with the ideal of minimal government.

Democracy and Ungovernability

The relation between liberalism and democracy has always been difficult: *nec cum te nec sine te*. Now that liberalism seems once again to come down to a defence of the minimal state (which is not to deny its consistency in this with the best liberal tradition), the relation is more vexed than ever. Of late, polemical discussion has revolved principally around the theme of ungovernability.[70] While in the early stages of the debate the main target, as we have seen, was the tyranny of the majority, which led liberals to defend at all costs the liberty of the individual against the invasions of the public sphere even where majority rule prevailed, nowadays the target is the inability of democratic governments to find suitable means of controlling conflict in complex societies – a target which reverses the signs, for it highlights the deficiency rather than the excess of power.

There are three main lines of argument put forward in support of the thesis that democratic regimes are inherently ungovernable:

(a) Democratic regimes, in contrast to autocratic ones, characteristically experience a growing disproportion between the demands emanating from civil society and the capacity of the system to respond (in the terminology of systems theory this is known as 'overload'). This supposed characteristic of democracies has two causes, opposite in nature but each tending to produce the same result. First of all, democratic government inherits from the liberal state a range of institutions, which are in fact (as we have noted) presuppositions of the effective functioning of popular power; these include freedom of assembly and association, the freedom of interest groups, trade unions and parties to organize, and the widest possible extension of political rights. By means of these institutions, individuals and groups are able to put their demands to the public powers knowing that the latter must see to their urgent satisfaction or else risk a loss of support. Pressure on such a scale is completely unknown in autocratic regimes, where the government controls the press, protest demonstrations are banned, trade unions are either disallowed or tolerated only as appendages of the political establishment, and the only political parties are those which either constitute the government or are a direct outgrowth of it. In the second place, in a democratic system with its procedures for collective decision-making and for responding to demands coming from civil society, decisions may be slow in being reached and on occasion indefinitely deferred on account of the network of interlocking powers of veto. In autocracies, by contrast, power is concentrated in a few hands or even in the single person of a charismatic leader whose word is law; there is no place for institutions such as parliaments in which various opinions are debated and decisions taken only after lengthy discussion (and even then parliamentary decisions may be subject in turn to the control of a jurisdictional body such as the constitutional court or to the views of the people themselves as expressed in a referendum). Autocracies are able to take swift, peremptory and definitive decisions. The contrast here can be summed up by saying that in a democracy it is easy to put demands but much harder to extract a response, whereas in an autocracy, it is difficult to make demands but responses to them are more readily agreed.

(b) Democratic regimes are more prone to social conflict than are autocratic regimes. Given that one task of whoever governs is to resolve social conflicts in such a way that individuals and groups representing different interests can live together peaceably, it is clear that the sharper the level of conflict, the harder it becomes to manage it. A pluralistic society of the kind which exists and flourishes in a democratic political system is beset by a multitude of contrary interests; class conflict is multiplied by a host of petty corporate squabbles; it becomes impossible to satisfy one interest without harming another, and this leads to an endless chain of aggravation. We know that the interests of particular parties ought to be subordinated to collective interests, but what precisely does this impressive formula mean? As a rule, the various component elements of a democratic government – a government in which the different parties must answer to their electors for the choices that they make – recognizes only one common interest, which is that they ought to satisfy those interests (partial interests, on many occasions) for whose satisfaction the greatest degree of consensus is forthcoming.

(c) In democratic regimes, power is more evenly distributed than in autocratic regimes; the former, unlike the latter, are characterized by what is nowadays referred to as 'diffusion' of power. One mark of a democratic society is that it has several centres of power (hence the appropriateness of the term 'polyarchy' in its application to democracies). The diffusion of power increases the more the government of society is regulated at every level by procedures that allow for participation and dissent, since these multiply the sites at which collective decisions are taken. Power in a democratic society is not only diffuse, but also fragmented and difficult to reintegrate. This fragmentation of power has evident negative consequences when it comes to the question of governability; fragmentation leads to a competition between different centres of power and in the long run creates conflict between the very subjects supposedly responsible for resolving them. The conflict is as it were raised to a higher power. A certain degree of social conflict is part of normal functioning, but a conflict of powers is pathological and so aggravates social conflict that it too ends by becoming pathological.

To deplore the ungovernability of democratic regimes is to be drawn towards authoritarian solutions. These have a double thrust: in the first place, executive power can be strengthened, and this represents a tendency to promote presidential or semi-presidential types of system over parliamentary governments of the classical kind; in the second place, the sphere of standard democratic decision-making in accordance with the principle of majority rule can be ever more narrowly circumscribed. If democracies do indeed find themselves suffering from 'overload', then there are in fact basically only two remedies available. Either one can improve the functioning of the organs of decision (the objective of moves to increase the power of government vis-à-vis parliament), or one can drastically reduce their power (the objective of proposals for limiting the power of the majority). Every actual democracy, unlike the Rousseauean ideal, came into being as a limited democracy, in the sense already explained; majority decisions were from the beginning denied any purchase on all questions affecting rights to liberty, which were regarded, precisely, as 'inviolable'. Among the proposals put forward by one group of neo-liberal writers has been the idea that constitutional limits should also be set on the economic and fiscal powers of parliament, with a view to preventing it from responding politically to social demands involving a level of public expenditure in excess of the resources of the country. Once again, the conflict between liberalism and democracy resolves itself into a situation wherein liberal doctrine, while accepting democracy as a method or set of 'rules of the game', wants at the same time to determine, when it sees a need, the limits within which these rules have application.

It was democracy which benefited most from the clash between liberal and democratic currents, when this made its first appearance during the last century: political discriminations were thereafter gradually but inexorably abolished and universal suffrage established. Today, democratic reaction to neo-liberalism centres on the demand that participation in collective decisions should be extended to matters and areas outside the political sphere. The aim is to win new opportunities and openings for popular participation, and thus to prepare the ground for the passage from what Macpherson, in his typology of the various stages of democratization, calls the phase of 'equilibrium democracy', to that of participatory democracy.[71]

To consider this constant dialectical interplay between liberalism and democracy in the perspective of general political theory is to realize that underlying the conflict between the liberals, with their demand that the state should govern as little as possible, and the democrats, with their demand that the government of the state should rest as far as possible in the hands of the citizens (a conflict which is being continually transferred to higher levels without attaining any definitive resolution), is a clash between two different understandings of liberty. These are usually termed negative liberty and positive liberty. Opposing judgements are made upon them, depending on historical circumstances, but depending above all on the social position of the judge; those who are well placed usually favour the former, those lower in the social scale usually opt for the latter. Since every hitherto existing society has contained members of both these categories, this wholesome dispute is not of a kind to be resolved once and for all, and insofar as it has from time to time issued in agreement, this has been in the nature of a compromise. Unfortunately, not all regimes have the benefit of this conflict, which is denied outlet where the first kind of liberty is usurped by unlimited power; or where the place of the second kind is usurped by a power without public accountability. Faced with either of these alternatives, these hostile twins, liberalism and democracy, of necessity become allies.

Notes

1. B. Constant, *De la liberté des anciens comparée à celle des modernes* (1818), in *Collection complète des ouvrages*, Béchet Libraire, Paris 1820, vol. 4, part 7, p. 253.

2. Ibid.

3. J.-J. Rousseau, *The Social Contract and Discourses*, vol. 1, p. 7, trans. and introd. G.D.H. Cole, London 1973, p. 176.

4. Ibid., p. 186.

5. Ibid.

6. J. Locke, *Two Treatises of Civil Government* (1690), Dent, London 1970, p. 119.

7. H. Bracton, *De legibus et consuetudinibus Angliae*, ed. G.E. Woodbine, Harvard University Press, Cambridge, Mass. 1968, vol. 2, p. 33.

8. Ulpiano, Dig., vol. 1, part 3, p. 31.

9. T. Paine, *Common Sense* (1776), Penguin, Harmondsworth 1976, p. 65.

10. I. Kant, *Über den Gemeinspruch: Das mag in der Theorie richtig sein, taugt aber nicht für die Praxis* (1793).

11. W. von Humboldt, *The Limits of State Action* (1792), Cambridge University Press, Cambridge 1969, pp. 20–21.

12. Ibid., p. 22.

13. Ibid., p. 65.

14. Ibid., p. 83.

15. Ibid., p. 24.

16. Ibid., p. 34.

17. Ibid., p. 35.

18. I. Kant, *Idee zu einer allgemeinen Geschichte in weltbürgerlicher Absicht* (1784).

19. Ibid.

20. N. Machiavelli, *The Prince*, trans. W.K. Marriott, Dent, London 1958, p. 22.

21. G.W.F. Hegel, *The Philosophy of History*, trans. J. Sibree, Dover, London 1956.

22. A. Hamilton, J. Madison, J. Jay, *The Federalist Papers* (1788), Mentor, London 1961, p. 71.

23. Ibid., p. 77.

24. J.-J. Rousseau, *The Social Contract*, p. 240.

25. Ibid., pp. 217–18.

26. Hamilton, Madison & Jay, *The Federalist Papers*, p. 82.

27. E. Burke, 'Speech at the Conclusion of the Poll on his being Declared Duly Elected' (1774), *The Works*, John C. Nimmo, London 1899, vol. 2, p. 96.

28. For a commentary on the theme, see P. Violante, *Lo spazio della rappresentanza. I Francia 1788–1789*, Palermo 1981.

29. Aristotle, *Politics* 1253a, trans. E. Barker, Clarendon Press, Oxford 1948, pp. 7–8.

30. B. Croce, *Storia d'Europa nel secolo decimonono*, Laterza, Bari 1932, p. 21.

31. See A.S.P. Woodhouse, ed., *Puritanism and Liberty, Being the Army Debates (1647–49) from the Clarke Manuscripts*, Dent, London 1986 pp. 356–7.

32. A. de Tocqueville, *Democracy in America* (1833–1840), trans. G. Lawrence, Fontana, London 1968, vol. 2, p. 898.

33. J.S. Mill, 'Tocqueville on Democracy in America', *London Review*, June–January 1835–36, pp. 85–129.

34. J.S. Mill, *Utilitarianism, Liberty, Representative Government*, Dent, London 1962, p. 277.

35. Cited in the Italian collection of Tocqueville's writing, D. Cofrancesco, ed. Guida, Naples 1971, p. 13.

36. Tocqueville, *Democracy in America*, vol. 1, p. 8.

37. Ibid., vol. 2, p. 650.

38. Ibid., vol. 1, p. 305.

39. Ibid., vol. 1, p. 311.

40. Ibid., vol. 2, pp. 899–900.

41. Ibid., vol. 2, p. 901.

42. Tocqueville, *Discours sur la révolution sociale* (1848).

43. J. Bentham, 'Anarchical Fallacies' in *The Works*, J. Bowring, ed., William Tait, Edinburgh, vol. 2, p. 500.

44. J.S. Mill, *Utilitarianism, Liberty, Representative Government*, p. 6.

45. Ibid., p. 16.

46. Ibid., p. 74.

47. Ibid., pp. 72–3.

48. Ibid., p. 74.

49. Ibid., p. 75.

50. Ibid., p. 73.

51. Ibid., p. 211.

52. Ibid., p. 279.

53. Ibid., p. 290.

54. Ibid., p. 268.

55. F. De Sanctis, *Letteratura e vita nazionale*, Einaudi, Turin 1950, p. 7.

56. F. De Sanctis, *Mazzini e la scuola democratica*, Einaudi, Turin 1951, p. 6.

57. Ibid., p. 13.

58. Ibid., p. 14.

59. Ibid., pp. 13–14.

60. The phrase is that used by R. Romeo in his *Cavour e il suo tempo. I, 1810–1842*, Laterza, Bari 1969, p. 288.

61. G. Mazzini, *I sistemi e la democrazia. Pensieri*, in *Mazzini*, G. Galasso, ed., Il Mulino, Bologna 1961, pp. 101–2.

62. Ibid., p. 110.

63. G. Mazzini, 'Lettera ai signori Tocqueville e Falloux ministri di Francia', in G. Mazzini, *Scritti Politici*, T. Grandi and A. Comba, eds., Utet, Turin 1972, p. 647.

64. G. Mazzini, *I sistemi e la democrazia*, p. 96.

65. R. Romeo, *Cavour e il suo tempo*, p. 288.

66. G. Mazzini, 'Dei doveri dell 'uomo', in *Scritti politici*, p. 847.

67. The exchange between Croce and Einaudi is to be found in the volume, *Liberismo e liberalismo*, P. Solari, ed., Ricciardi, Naples 1957. The praise for Hobhouse is to be found in the first of these writings: 'La concezione liberale come concezione della vita' (1927), p. 14.

68. F. von Hayek, 'Liberalismo' in *Enciclopedia del Novecento*, Istituto dell 'Enciclopedia italiana, Rome 1978, vol. 3, p. 990.

69. For an assessment of this debate together with bibliographical details, see F. Comanducci, 'La meta-utopia di Nozick' in *Materiali per una storia della cultura giuridica*, vol. 12, 1982, pp. 507–23.

70. The debate on the ungovernability of democratic regimes arose initially in response to the writings collected together in M. Crozier, S.P. Huntingdon, J. Watanuki, *The Crisis of Democracy: Report on the Governability of Democracy*, New York 1975.

71. C.B. Macpherson, *The Life and Time of Liberal Democracy*, Oxford University Press, Oxford 1977. According to the author, there are four stages in the development of democracy: protective democracy, development democracy, equilibrium democracy, and lastly (and as yet unrealized) participatory democracy.

AVAILABLE IN THE RADICAL THINKERS SERIES

Minima Moralia:
Reflections on a
Damaged Life

THEODOR ADORNO

Paperback 1 84467 051 1
$12/£6/$14CAN
256 pages • 5 x 7.75 inches

For Marx

LOUIS ALTHUSSER

Paperback 1 84467 052 X
$12/£6/$14CAN
272 pages • 5 x 7.75 inches

The System of Objects

JEAN BAUDRILLARD

Paperback 1 84467 053 8
$12/£6/$14CAN
224 pages • 5 x 7.75 inches

Liberalism and Democracy

NORBERTO BOBBIO

Paperback 1 84467 062 7
$12/£6/$14CAN
112 pages • 5 x 7.75 inches

AVAILABLE IN THE RADICAL THINKERS SERIES

The Politics of Friendship
JACQUES DERRIDA

Paperback 1 84467 054 6
$12/£6/$14CAN
320 pages • 5 x 7.75 inches

The Function of Criticism
TERRY EAGLETON

Paperback 1 84467 055 4
$12/£6/$14CAN
136 pages • 5 x 7.75 inches

Signs Taken for Wonders:
On the Sociology of Literary
Forms

FRANCO MORETTI

Paperback 1 84467 056 2
$12/£6/$14CAN
288 pages • 5 x 7.75 inches

The Return of the Political
CHANTAL MOUFFE

Paperback 1 84467 057 0
$12/£6/$14CAN
176 pages • 5 x 7.75 inches

AVAILABLE IN THE RADICAL THINKERS SERIES

Sexuality in the Field
of Vision

JACQUELINE ROSE

Paperback 1 84467 058 9
$12/£6/$14CAN
272 pages • 5 x 7.75 inches

The Information Bomb

PAUL VIRILIO

Paperback 1 84467 059 7
$12/£6/$14CAN
160 pages • 5 x 7.75 inches

Culture and Materialism

RAYMOND WILLIAMS

Paperback 1 84467 060 0
$12/£6/$14CAN
288 pages • 5 x 7.75 inches

The Metastases of
Enjoyment:
Six Essays on Women and
Causality

SLAVOJ ŽIŽEK

Paperback 1 84467 061 9
$12/£6/$14CAN
240 pages • 5 x 7.75 inches